To Sandy
with ble.....
the Grail Maidens of the
new Camelot

London's Camelot and The Secrets of The Grail

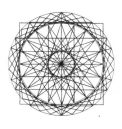

Earthstars Publishing. London N14 6LP

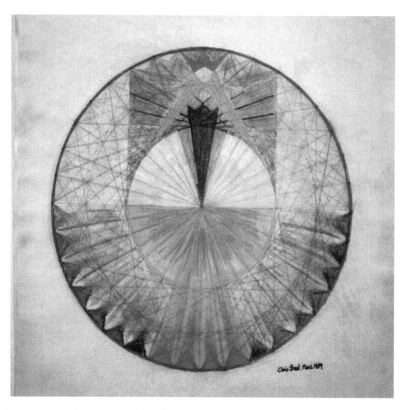

Front cover illustration, "The Goddess and the Grail" by Chris Street, 1989.

LONDON'S CAMELOT
AND
THE SECRETS
OF
THE GRAIL

C.E.STREET

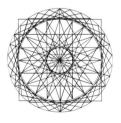

Earthstars Publishing. London N14 6LP

By the same author:

Earthstars. (1990) Hermitage Publishing.
The first book this century to mention Camelot Moat

Earthstars The Visionary Landscape (2000)
Hermitage Pubishing

The Beer Guru's Guide (2006) Souvenir press.

See www.earthstars.co.uk for further information

A CIP catalogue record for this book is available from The British Library.

ISBN: 978-0-9515967 - 3 - 9

First published Midsummer Solstice June 2009.

Illustrations

CONTENTS

INTRODUCTION

Many places have been put forward as the location for King Arthur's Camelot. Sir Thomas Mallory, in his **Morte D'Arthur** (first printed in 1485), seemed firmly convinced that Camelot had been Winchester. It was, after all, the capital of the West Saxon Kings and after Egbert the first king of all England was crowned there in 827, it became England's most important city until the eleventh century when William the Conqueror's rule commenced.

Mallory's printer, Caxton, clearly disagreed. In his own notes added to Mallory's book, he expressed the firm belief that Camelot was in Wales. It is generally assumed he meant Caerleon, the City of Legions, which had been mentioned by Geoffrey of Monmouth in his **Historia Regum Britanniae (History of The Kings of Britain)**, written around 1136. Geoffrey never actually calls Caerleon Camelot, but does state that it was the site of Arthur's Coronation.

Popular myth adds yet another location to the selection and places Camelot on the rocky headland of Tintagel in Cornwall, whilst John Leland, Henry VIII's antiquarian, was the first to associate Camelot with the iron-age hill fort in Somerset known as Cadbury Castle. Leland's reference to Camelot clearly stems from a piece of local folk-lore:

"At South-Cadbyri standeth Camallate, sometime a famous town or castle. The people can tell nothing there but that they have heard say Arthur much resorted to Camalat."

On the opposite side of the country, there's another strong contender. Colchester in Essex can lay claim to the name and fame and back it up with some convincing evidence. Its pre-Roman name seems to have been a Celtic version of Camelot – Camulodunon, later Romanised to Camulodunum.

This is said to mean the stronghold or fort (dunum) of Camulus (the Celtic god of war) and, although in the territory of the Trinovante

1

tribe, this was the seat from where Cunobelinus (Shakespeare's Cymbeline) the King of the Cattuvellaunii, ruled much of England. This previous use as a seat of power was probably why the Romans chose to use it as their first capital until Boudicca burnt it to the ground in her valiant attempt to win back England from Rome's occupying forces.

Dr. John Morris, an English historian who specialised in the study of the history of Sub-Roman Britain, suggested in his book "**The Age of Arthur**" (1973) that the descendents of Romanised Britons might have looked back to a golden age of peace and prosperity under Roman rule and therefore the name 'Camelot' of Arthurian legend may have been a reference to the capital of Britanria in Roman times, Camulodunum.

The present name Colchester comes from the Saxons, who called the town Colne Ceaster. It simply means castle on the river Cole.

So there we have the five main contenders for the title: Caerleon, Winchester, Cadbury Castle, Tintagel and Colchester.

Surprisingly, there is another and its earliest records show that it has actually been called Camelot from at least a generation before Mallory's **Morte D'Arthur** popularised the Arthurian legends in Britain. That's nowhere near as early as Colchester's claim to the title, I admit, but it does amount to almost 600 years, during which time, you'd think the place and name would have attracted some attention.

But no, it has been overlooked, forgotten and shrouded in obscurity for over half a millenium.

In fact, with the publication of my first book, Earthstars, in 1990, I seem to have been the first person to bring this interesting and unusual site into the public spotlight in the 20th Century.

Actually, its almost total lack of public awareness is quite remarkable when you consider that this Camelot is on the outskirts of Britain's most heavily populated city and is as much a place of mystery and magic as the legendary Camelot.

It is reputedly haunted by a Norman robber baron and closely associated with several Kings of England. It's a place where a mysterious treasure is reputed to have been buried, where visions and other paranormal phenomena are reported, where mysterious ley-lines and Earth energies form a major junction point and a spot where modern witches, druids and other mystics of many spiritual paths are drawn to experience the magical atmosphere of the place.

It also has some rather strange and intriguing associations with The Arthurian legends and the Grail myths.

On top of these facts, I add the belief that the place was originally some kind of oracular shrine and place of vision.

Since it is the Grail's tendency to appear in a vision rather than as a solid and tangible reality, I believe this may be the location of an other-wordly Grail Castle; where one may be granted a vision of the Holy Grail, but that's only my personal opinion, read on and judge for yourself.

CHAPTER ONE

WHO CALLED IT CAMELOT ?
ORIGINS OF THE NAME.

Camlet Moat nestles in woodland on the northern edge of Trent Park in Cockfosters. It is a square secluded isle about 60 yards wide and can only be reached via a single crossing point on the eastern side.

Casual visitors to the park may never notice it. It is set back from the nearest path and is one of those magical places that can be virtually invisible to those whose presence it doesn't wish to encourage within its precincts.

To others, it exerts a flame and moth relationship, irresistibly drawing people to it so they may experience something of its mystery for themselves.

The name Camlet is an abbreviation. In days gone by it was definitely known as Camelot and there is plenty of hard evidence to prove the fact.

On a map of the area dating from 1658 (copies available from the records' office in Kew), there is no possible chance of mistaking or missing the name because it was not just the moat that was called Camelot. The name is emblazoned upon the entire landscape around it.

According to the map, Camelot Moat occupied a prime location upon the summit of Camelot Hill and was clearly a centre of some influence since it was surrounded on all sides by four larger areas, all bearing the same name: East Camelot, South Camelot, West Camelot and North Camelot.

Camelot was therefore not just a single, small, moated isle. It was an important and sizeable domain of several acres with the moat at its centre. Interestingly, the whole area was divided into the four quar-

4

ters which normally form the traditional divisions of a Holy City and the basis of an ancient sacred site.

On the same map (and others), a road called Camlet Way runs roughly east-west, on the north side of the moat and presumably, it was called Camlet Way because it led to this specific place.

It stills exists as a road, but where it originally began is lost in antiquity. These days, the name Camlet Way is only found in a short section which starts two miles west, near The Parish Church of St. Mary the Virgin at Monken Hadley. From there, it runs through Hadley Wood where it has become Beech Hill, then Ferny Hill and finally, Hadley Road. By the look of the old maps it may once have continued all the way into Enfield Town.

How old this route is, no one knows, though a clue could be contained in the term "Way" which commonly denotes a Roman Road, as in The Icknield Way, The Appian Way or The Fosse Way. The word "Way" itself derives from the Roman "via" or "viae" (plural). So, if this is correct, Camlet Way may be up to 2,000 years old. Even older if you subscribe to the belief that the Roman roads were often built upon existing unpaved British trackways and routes. Molmutius, King of Britain in around 500BC is actually credited with creating our first roads.

As we'll see in later chapters, Roman artefacts have been found here, so by association, London's Camelot may have been occupied during that era, if not before.

So what do we know about this place and its origins ? First, local folklore places Camelot Moat in a timescale dating back nearly 1000 years.

According to the respected local historian David Pam, in his book **The History of Enfield Chase**, a survey of the area conducted between 1656 and 1658 states that the name Camelot dates from at least the 12th Century when the site was the location for the Manor House of Sir Geoffrey De Mandeville, Earl of Essex.

"The Manor and Chase of Enfield were anciently in the possession of Geoffrey de Mandeville in the reign of William the Conqueror, whose seat and habitation at that time, called Camelot, was situated on the chase near unto Potter's Lodge, the ruins whereof are yet remaining and being moated is to this day called Camelot Moat."

The last Sir Geoffrey de Mandeville died in 1144, so if he was responsible for naming his Manor Camelot, he predates the earliest mention of it in literature by 30 years. According to the author Graham Phillips, the name Camelot is first mentioned in the romances written by the French poet Chretian de Troyes between 1170 and 1185. It's a very brief mention, too.

" Upon a certain Ascension Day, King Arthur had come from Caerleon and had held a very magnificent court at Camelot as was fitting on such a day."

Clearly he didn't think Caerleon was Camelot.

But if this hilltop moat and its surroundings were really known as Camelot thirty years before the name had appeared in any Arthurian romance, it raises the interesting possibility that the name here could be of unique and genuine antiquity.

This view is supported by David Avery in his booklet **Saxon Enfield: The Place Name Evidence.** Mr. Avery states that there is **"no doubt that it (Camlet) was originally Camelot"** and that the name **"is indisputably Celtic."**

The etymology, he explains, stems from three words, cam, meaning crooked or wandering, el meaning stream or river and Lot or lod, meaning place.

Ironically, the earliest reference to Camelot in the local vicinity, dates from 1439 when the "Manor of Camelot" was demolished and its residue sold to help pay for the cost of rebuilding Hertford Castle. David Pam's book informs us:

"In May 1439, instructions were issued that the Manor of Camelot should be taken down and the materials sold and the money employed towards the repair of Hertford castle."

Despite the fact that this clearly refers to Camelot Manor, there is some dispute amongst local historians whether a manor house actually stood here.

Most prefer to support the notion that it was a less prestigous lodge. Mr Avery quotes a reference in 1441 to the *"logii de Camelot" The Lodge of Camelot*. But if Camelot Manor was demolished in 1439, then the lodge mentioned in 1441 must have replaced it.

Possibly the demolition of Camelot Manor might suggest that, by those times, it had fallen into disrepair and was considered of little importance, thus commencing the spiral into the obscurity it has endured until recent times.

It's not entirely clear who actually lived at Camelot Manor at the time of its demolition. It seems to have been owned by Henry VI who ruled from 1422-1461, but it is hardly likely he lived there.

From 1266 to 1421 it appears to have been in the possession of a succession of Humphreys, all members of the de Bohun family, descendants of the de Mandevilles.

In fact, one Humphrey de Bohun is on record as having procured from the King permission to fortify and crenelate his manor house at Enfield in 1347 (from a mss in The British Museum).

By 1421, following the death of yet another Humphrey de Bohun, the Manor of Enfield was assigned in purpory to the King (Henry V) who in 1422 granted it to Queen Catherine in dower. The Manor then remained with the Duchy of Lancaster for several years being granted to various privileged relatives of royalty, including Margaret of Anjou, wife of Henry VI, Elizabeth Woodville, wife of Edward IV, and Elizabeth, sister of Edward VI.

The demolition of Camelot Manor in 1439, means that The Manor of Enfield referred to in these records, may not relate to Camelot Manor after that date.

It is believed that the location of this later Manor is the site of the 'palace' which stood in Enfield Town near the market place and is now the Palace Gardens Shopping Centre.

In researching this, I was amazed to find that this now obscure and relatively unknown Camelot seems to previously have had extremely strong connections to families of Royal descent and was clearly well-known to many Kings, even if the legendary Arthur was conspicuously absent from the list.

The original 'Lord of the Manor' in this area prior to the Norman Conquest, was Ansgar (sometimes spelled Asgar), Staller to the King (Harold). The Staller was the King's right-hand man. Some writers claim he was also Constable of the Tower of London (**The Mediaeval Castle** by Norman John Greville Pounds).

Sir Geoffrey de Mandeville was awarded Ansgar's lands, Manor and offices. He was a key player in the rivalry between King Stephen (William's grandson) and Matilda (his cousin) and was grandson to an earlier Geoffrey de Mandeville who had been one of William's right hand men. The two Geoffrey de Mandevilles are often confused, but it was this later one who was created Earl of Essex in 1141, by King Stephen, in order to secure his services in the war with Empress Matilda.

De Mandeville's descendants, the De Bohuns were always well-connected and well-known in the upper echelons of society. They married into the royal line.

In 1380 at Arundel Castle, Mary de Bohun, daughter of one of the long line of Humphreys, married Henry Bollingbrook who, 19 years later, became Henry IV.

It must have been a happy marriage. They had seven children, one of whom became Henry V.

8

So, far from being an obscure and insignificant location, as it is today, Camlet Moat with its fortified Manor House was once a grand and important place, home to members of the ruling classes and frequented regularly by Royalty.

It may also have occupied a strategic position in the military sense.

At least one local historian, Dr. Stephen Doree in **The Origins of the Edmonton Hundred**, has suggested that Asgar's and De Mandeville's role as Constable of the Tower reflected the importance of their manors (which included Enfield and Edmonton) to the outer, northern defences of London.

Asgar, as Staller to the King, was in fact directly responsible for the defence of London. In support of this fact, it is said that he led an army of men from London to fight against William of Normandy in 1066.

More important, if it really was a strategic position of military significance, any King in the role of warlord, as Arthur was, would certainly have been aware of the place.

Another local historian, Jenny Lee Cobham, expands on this in her thoroughly well-researched book, **Geoffrey De Mandeville and London's Camelot** (1997);

" In other words, Camelot moat lay in an area which had probably been very important to London since Roman times. If this is the case, then it is just possible that Camlet Moat and its environs may have been occupied since Roman times. I hesitate to suggest it as a villa site, but this remains a remote possibility, as it also remains a possibility that the site has been in use since pre-Roman times. The word Camelot apparently contains a Celtic element and so this may be a very ancient site indeed."

Certainly, some Roman remains have been unearthed at Camlet Moat. Sir Phillip Sassoon, the last private owner of Trent Park, conducted an archaeological excavation of the moat in 1923 and reported finds that included a pair of Roman shoes and Roman daggers. In addition, Barnet museum's records show that a Mr C. Houston sent them four Roman coins dating from the fourth century, explaining that he had found them in Trent Park where the moat is located.

Where any of these finds are these days is a mystery, but if they are genuine, and there is no reason to suppose they are not, it is likely something existed on the site of Camelot Moat way back during the Roman occupation, or before.

What it was, is anyone's guess. There is no clear cut indication of anything specific.

Significantly though, as Jenny Lee Cobham said, it does leave the possibility that the site of Camelot Moat was occupied continuously from the Roman era or earlier, which would include the fifth or sixth centuries, the correct timescale to be contemporary with a real King Arthur, if there ever was one.

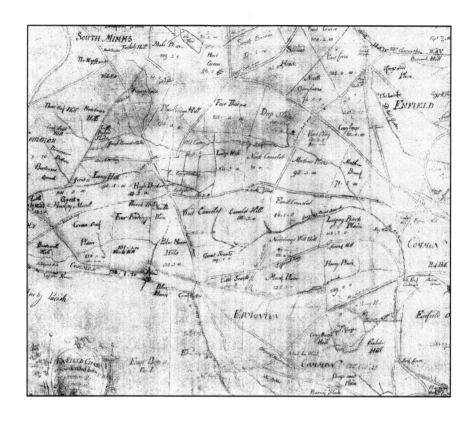

Illustration 1: 1658 map showing Camelot Moat, Camelot Hill, East Camelot, West Camelot and North Camelot.

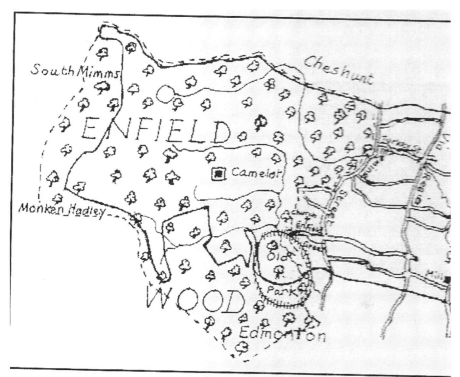

Enfield towards the middle of the Twelfth Century.
On this map, the parish-boundary is shown as an unbroken thick black lin
and the probable limits of Enfield Wood (much of which was incorporat
into Enfield Close in about 1140) by a broken line.

**Illustration 2: Enfield towards the middle of the twelfth Century, reproduced
from David Avery's booklet on Saxon Enfield.**

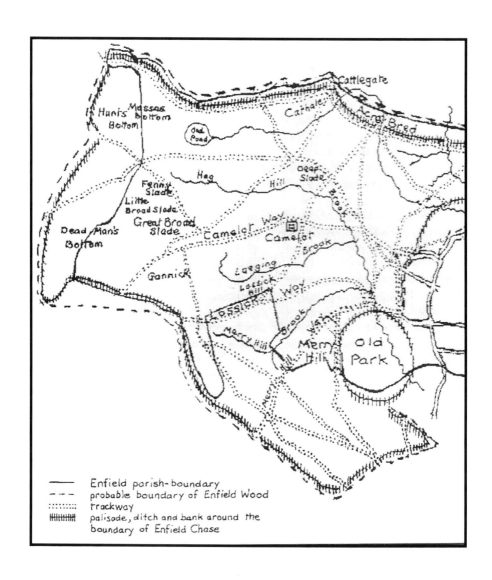

Illustration 3: Another map from David Avery's booklet, showing paths, boundaries and tracks through the early Enfield Chase. Both maps show Camelot Moat as a prominent feature of the Royal Hunting Ground.

CHAPTER TWO

THE SECRET TRADITION
IN ARTHURIAN LEGEND

Around the time I was delving into the mysteries of this moated isle, I found an interesting book, **The Secret Tradition in Arthurian Legend**. It had been written by Gareth Knight, a well-known mystic who had been one of the leading figures within Dion Fortune's Society of the Inner Light, a School of the Western Mystery Tradition.

He presents the Arthurian characters as living archetypes which form the basis of a workable mystery school system, comprised of three primary grades.

First is the grade of the Powers of Arthur, enshrined in the concept of chivalry and relating to loyalty, dedication and service to "The Lady".

Second is the grade of the Powers of Merlin, bringing knowledge of invisible forces that are the true source of causation within the material world.

The final grade is of the Powers of Guinevere, which Mr. Knight suggests is based upon forces of polarity within the aura.

I believe this latter grade clearly conceals a deeper mystery since the name Guinevere itself literally means 'The bright animating spirit of life'.

To my mind, Guinevere represents an ancient goddess figure, who is an anthropomorphised aspect of the universal and planetary life force. The etymology stems from gwen – Welsh for white - and from the old druidic term for the life force, nwevre, from which we get the French vivre, the mythical creature the wyvern and possibly the concept of the "weaver" of the web of life.

To underline a connection to goddess figures, Gwener in Welsh, of course, also means Venus and relates to the planet, the goddess and her sacred day, Friday.

Others with a more mundane perspective on these issues may disagree. The name Guinevere is usually translated simply as meaning 'white and smooth.'

What first caught my attention in this book, though, was a map. A map of Europe showing Camelot, not in Wales and not near Colchester, Winchester, Somerset or Tintangel.

This map clearly placed Camelot in the area of North London.

Now that is what I call a meaningful synchronicity. Far too much of a coincidence to be a coincidence.

Overlaid on the map was the outline of a Goddess called Brisen, as aspect of the ancient British Goddess Bride (often also known as Bridget) who equates with Robert Graves' White Goddess.

Her body stretched across Europe whilst her head fell over Britain with Camelot near her mouth, Jerusalem at her groin and Byzantium near her navel.

Britain was marked as Logres, the name of King Arthur's legendary realm in the Matter of Britain. According to Wikipedia, it derives from the Welsh word Lloegr, a name of uncertain origin simply meaning 'England.'

She was obviously meant to represent the feminine spirit of the land, the hidden goddess, in the same way that I thought Guinevere does. A key to understanding the deeper secret tradition in the Arthurian legends is that the 'Lady' that the knights serve is actually the spirit or soul of the land, embodied by a pre-Christian goddess of sovereignty.

That is why many goddess archetypes have different aspects, each relating to her changing role throughout the seasons and cycles of our little planet. The virgin maiden of spring. The desirable goddess of love and summer. The fruitful mother of autumn and the hag of winter.

The map had been reproduced from a book by the poet Charles Williams; **Taliessin through Logres, The Region of the Summer Stars.**

Taliessin is a character from Welsh folklore, a visionary bard, strongly linked to Arthurian legend and some claim, contemporary with Merlin and Arthur.

So why would an early 20th century poet like Charles Williams have placed Camelot in London? Did he know the actual site of Camelot Moat? Was he familiar with it ?

Williams grew up in London (and later in St. Albans), within easy reach of the Cockfosters/Enfield area where the moat is located, but back in his day, it was on private property. Not openly accessible to the public as it is now. Any suggestion that he knew the place would be sheer speculation.

I decided to contact Gareth Knight, who had been my tarot tutor, to ask him if he knew why Charles Williams may have placed Camelot in this location. Gareth's reply was that Williams probably wasn't aware of the moat and it was more likely that he regarded London itself as Camelot.

Why Williams should believe this is not easily explained, but it's obvious from his poetry that he did. There is a line in Taliessin through Logres which confirms Gareth's opinion.

"Through Camelot,
which is London in Logres,
by Paul and Arthur's door,
Taliessin came
to the School of the Poets."

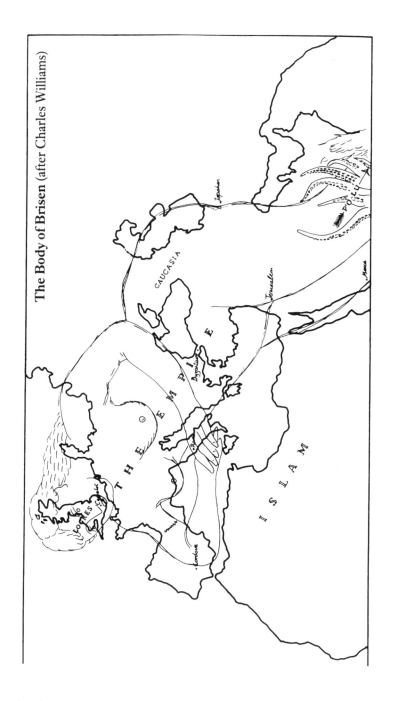

The Body of Brisen (after Charles Williams)

Illustration 4:
Charles Williams' map showing Camelot in the location of London.

He couldn't have stated it clearer. For him, Camelot is London in Logres.

If the reference to Paul means St. Paul's Cathedral, it seems that there is a connection to Arthur and his sagas, there too, but we will come to that later.

For much of his life, Charles Williams was employed in the publishing industry by Oxford University Press and was an important member of the literary group, The Inklings. He numbered C.S. Lewis and J.R.R. "Tollers" Tolkien amongst his closest friends.

He was a very intelligent, popular and discerning man. So if he believed London was somehow associated with Camelot, he must had had good reason. I suspect the answer lies in his mystical inclinations.

Despite being a devout Anglican, Williams had extensive knowledge of the Tarot, the Kabbala, and in common with W.B. Yeats, Arthur Machen and the notorious Aleister Crowley, was for a while, a member of the pre-eminent occult "secret" society of his times, The Hermetic Order of The Golden Dawn.

Actually, for a secret society, it seems to have been extremely well-known in certain circles.

I am not entirely familiar with what its members practised, but believe it involved a mixture of the Jewish mystical tradition of the Kabbala, the teachings of Hermes Trimegistus, the mysteries behind the Tarot, the Christian mysticism of the Rosicrucians, plus, if the photographs of Crowley's regalia are anything to go by, a heavy layer of Egyptian symbolism or ritual magic (though that might have just been him).

Charles Williams doesn't seem to have been a member of this exclusive society for very long. For whatever reasons, he decided The Golden Dawn wasn't for him and transferred his allegiance to A.E. Waite's Fraternity of the Rosy Cross, another Rosicrucian-based group, probably with very similar aims and practices.

Since the Matter of Britain and the Secret Tradition in Arthurian Legend frequently form an important study area in lyceums and societies of The Western Mystery Traditions, it is likely that Charles Williams' notions about Camelot stem from these.

If this is correct, it certainly raises a lot of questions about London's Camelot on Enfield Chase. Was this a location known to other members of these "secret" orders?

Was any owner of Trent Park, where the moat is located, a member of such a society ? Did Camlet Moat play a role in these traditions, as a location for ceremony, or initiation ? We don't know the answer to these questions for sure, but I personally suspect it did.

As we'll see in later chapters, it's definitely a place used for ceremonies and initiation today and local folk-lore suggests it may have been in the past.

CHAPTER THREE

KING ARTHUR'S CROSS

The mysterious map is typical of the strange synchronicities that began to occur around the time I was drawn to investigate Camelot Moat.

Another is the case of King Arthur's Cross. On 17th December 1981, The Enfield Advertiser ran a story that a local man, Derek Mahoney, had found the cross which had graced King Arthur's Tomb at Glastonbury Abbey.

The original cross had been first unearthed by the monks of the Abbey in 1191 and carried an inscription in Latin:

HIC JACET SEPULTUS INCLYTUS REX ARTHURUS IN INSULA AVALONIA - Here lies buried the renowned King Arthur on the Isle of Avalon.

The one Mr. Mahoney claimed to have found was identical. Did he find it in the Isle of Avalon, or the Somerset levels? No. He claimed to have picked it up in Enfield, just a couple of miles away from Camelot Moat.

According to the article, the cross was found in the grounds of Forty Hall, near "Maiden's Bridge" amongst mud that had been dredged from a nearby lake by council workmen.

Mr. Mahoney took it to the British Museum for examination where it was photographed. Unfortunately, the museum staff on duty that day lacked the expertise to assess whether it was genuine or a later copy and Mr Mahoney refused to leave it with them for further investigation.

Events then took a sad turn. Enfield council claimed that, as the cross had been found on their property, they were the rightful owners. They demanded that Mr. Mahoney hand it over to them.

Illustration 5:
The cross said to have been found on King Arthur's tomb in the grounds of
Glastonbury Abbey. An identical one was also found in 1980 in Enfield a mere
two miles from Camelot Moat.

Derek Mahoney was having none of that. He claimed this legendary artefact had fallen into his possession by the hand of fate and that he was the rightful owner. He refused to hand it over and promptly concealed it elsewhere in the local landscape. As a direct result, he was charged with Contempt of Court and sentenced to two years in Pentonville Prison.

Suspicions that the cross might be a fake were aroused when it came to light that Mahoney had been a mold maker for a well-known toy firm. It turned out that he was experienced in creating items from lead molds and that making a copy of The Glastonbury Cross would have been a fairly easy task for him.

For many, that explained the entire incident. Yet I'm not so sure.

What it doesn't explain is why Derek Mahoney chose to go to prison for something that was a worthless fake. As far as I can see, that's as big a mystery as the authenticity of the cross. I can only assume he endured his unnecessary incarceration in Pentonville because he actually believed the cross was the genuine article.

Actually, there's a slim possibility it could be genuine if we are to believe his account of how the item found its way into a North London lake.

The explanation can be found on-line in the notes of a meeting of The Enfield Archaeological Society in 1998.

Geoffrey Gillam, probably Enfield's leading local historian, explained that the earliest illustration of the cross had appeared in William Camden's **Brittannia**, first published in 1586. A later copy of the book had been produced at the end of the 18th Century by Richard Gough, who lived near Forty Hall.

Derek Mahoney had told Mr. Gillam that he thought Richard Gough had ordered a copy of the cross to be made to provide an illustration for the book and that somehow it had found its way into the lake.

To those who thought Mahoney had perpetrated a clever hoax, this falls under the dismissive heading of 'a likely story'. Particularly when you consider that Gough was a keen collector of antiquities and the cross is not amongst the list of his possessions, currently on file at the Bodleian Library, Oxford. Also, the lake was not on his property and his house was a good distance from it, which still leaves the question of how the cross came to end up there.

The whole affair is one mystery after another.

It ended tragically when Derek Mahoney took his own life. He never revealed where he had hidden the cross, so unless it turns up again, its authenticity or origins can never now be confirmed.

It is still concealed somewhere in the local landscape. Whether its whereabouts are discovered by someone else, as Mr. Mahoney himself said, is a matter of nemesis, fate.

All the unanswered questions surrounding it will remain just that. Unanswered.

Nevertheless, it did add to the growing list of curious Arthurian synchronicities that had come to light since my interest in Camelot Moat had been aroused.

CHAPTER FOUR

DIGGING UP SOME HARD EVIDENCE

There have been two main attempts to unearth the secrets and history of Camelot Moat. One by the Bevan family sometime in the 1880s. The other by Sir Phillip Sassoon in 1923. Let's start with the Bevans.

Robert Cooper Lee Bevan owned Trent Park from 1833 until his death in 1890. He personally had little or no interest in Camlet Moat which lay hidden in over-grown and secluded woodland on the northern boundary of his property. His wife, on the other hand, was fascinated by history and archaeology and she became determined to delve into the mysteries of the moat, enlisting the enthusiastic help of her daughter Nesta.

We would probably never had heard of these endeavours had not Nesta decided to publish an autobiography over sixty years later. It was titled **Spacious Days** and in it, many details of the rather amateurish excavations were revealed.

"A whole dungeon, with a chain attached to the wall, we dug out." Nesta Webster, nee Bevan, 1943.

This account from Spacious Days (also reproduced in Jenny Lee Cobham's book about Sir Geoffrey De Mandeville) tells a fairly complete tale of the excavations.

" the Rough Lot, was to me filled with romance, for there, surrounded by these venerable giants, amid the high stems of bracken, lay the circle of green and slimy water, thick with weeds, which once had formed the moat of Camlet Castle, home of the de Mandevilles. My mother, who loved archaeology, looked up its history in various old chronicles, and found that during the War of the Roses, the castle

had been attacked, and to save it from falling into the hands of their enemies, the de Mandevilles had taken their chest full of treasure and dropped it to the bottom of the well afterwards burning down the castle.

My mother felt sure that much of interest was to be found beneath the ground and she begged my father to begin excavations. He, however, was incredulous and only laughed at her enthusiasm. "You would find nothing there," he said.

" Then I will go and dig myself, " my mother answered firmly, and calling Edith and me - then about thirteen and ten - to join her, set forth one summer afternoon, armed with spades and bill hooks, to the Rough Lot.

The first thing was to cut away the brambles and the brushwood with which the whole island, surrounded by the moat, was overgrown, and after clearing a small space, we began to dig. I shall never forget the thrill when, after about an hour, we came upon the red tiles of the roof.

By this time, we were all three too tired to go on, and returned triumphant to the house to tell my father that "mamma had been right" and there was something to be found there. Papa, though still somewhat sceptical, then allowed some of the estate labourers to come and help us with the heavier digging and before long a number of interesting discoveries were brought to light.

A whole dungeon, with a chain attached to the wall, was dug out, also some oak of the drawbridge now turned black as ebony, sunk in the slime of the moat; in the course of time no doubt the portcullis might have been found. A quantity of small finds were also made – glazed tiles adorned with knights on horseback, silver coins of Edward IV, a lady's thimble, quite unlike the modern variety and covering only the tip of the finger, and so on.

But the chest of treasure was never found, for it was at this juncture my father died and my Brother Frank, who inherited Trent Park, cared even less about archaeological excavations, so those we had made were left to be filled in by fallen earth and the network of brambles soon covered them until no trace of our labours remained. Thus Camlet holds its secrets still."

For a bunch of amateurs and a couple of schoolgirls led by their mother, they seemed to have found quite a lot: A castle drawbridge.

A dungeon. Mediaeval glazed floor tiles. Red roof tiles. Coins from the reign of Edward IV. A well. So what can we learn from them ?

Well, the first thing we learn is that the Bevans refer to the place not simply as a moat or a Manor, but as a Castle. Perhaps that was how it was described in the *"various old chronicles"* Mrs. Bevan had used for her research. Perhaps it was her a romantic perspective on the old place.

Or perhaps it stemmed from the discovery of the drawbridge coupled with the reasonable assumption that anything with a drawbridge must be a castle.

The drawbridge itself must have been a sizeable affair, if the proportions of its timber (at least a foot square) are anything to go by. A small part of its oak frame has been dendro-chronologically dated to 1357, just ten years after one of the Humphrey de Bohuns had fortified his Manor. Given that there is likely to be a degree of error in the dating process (dendro-chronologically dated simply means someone counted or estimated the number of rings in the tree's trunk) there's a distinct possibility that the hefty drawbridge could have been a part of his fortifications.

Sadly, the idea that it could have been burnt down during the War of the Roses, and that Geoffrey de Mandeville could have hidden a treasure chest in the well can be safely filed under T for tosh. If Camelot Manor was demolished in 1439, it would not have been there to burn down in The War of The Roses. That didn't start until 1453. Nor would De Mandeville have been around at that time to hide his treasure in the well. He had died nearly four hundred years earlier.

If anything burnt down in the War of the Roses, it would have to have been a later structure, possibly the hunting lodge which is rumoured to have been built on the site.

The coins found also date from a period after the demolition of the Manor. Edward IV's reign did not begin until 1461.

It's worth noting though, that The War of the Roses was still in progress at that date and one of its major conflicts took place within walking distance of Camlet Moat during Edward IV's reign. The Battle of Barnet in 1471.

Edward IV himself was actually in the area leading his forces. The battle took place in heavy fog and spread over a wide area, after the routed forces of The Earl of Warwick fled into the nearby woodland. There is a distinct possibility that Camlet Moat could somehow have been involved in the fighting. So there may be an element of truth in that aspect of the tale.

What about the dungeon, the well and the tiles ?

The dungeon is fascinating. With a chain attached to the wall, there is no need to embellish schoolgirl imaginations. It must have been a dungeon. Why else would there be a chain ? Well, it was some sort of subterranean room anyway. It's probably still there somewhere waiting to be rediscovered. The mud and brambles and scattered fragments of red roof tiles certainly are, and so is the well, on the north-east corner of the moat's island, though with no sign of de Mandeville's chest of treasure. These days it is no more than a deep hole, half filled with water.

Tales of treasure, whether buried or hidden in a well, exert a powerful pull on the human imagination.

This one merits closer examination and its own chapter, so temporarily curb your curiosity.

That just leaves the thimble and glazed tiles. According to local historians, they were typical of the mediaeval period and don't really tell us anything we didn't already know.

Where any of these finds are today is as much a mystery as the origins of the moat. As far as we know, they were never handed to a museum for assessment, nor recorded, other than in **Spacious Days,** Nesta Bevan's autobiography.

Without that, we would never have known about the excavation and its discoveries at all, even if they didn't really add much to our knowledge of Camelot Moat.

Nesta was right.

" Camlet holds its secrets still."

CHAPTER FIVE

SIR PHILLIP SASSOON'S EXCAVATIONS

Sir Phillip Sassoon was a direct descendant of Mayer Amschel Rothschild, the founder of the dynasty. He was an advisor to Lloyd George, a one-time Minister for Air, and the last private owner of Trent Park.

Under his ownership, Trent Park was the hub of a dizzy social whirl into which celebrities, landed gentry, politicians, power brokers and the downright filthy rich of the era were drawn.

His interest in the rewards and excitement of archaeology seem likely to have been inspired by his visit to Egypt in 1923, where, according to The Barnet Press of 23/2/1923;

"(he) spent some time in archaeological research with the late Lord Carnavon and Howard Carter in The Valley of the Kings."

In actual fact, Sassoon had been present at the opening of Tutankhamen's tomb in February 1923 and must have been extremely impressed by the occasion and by the plethora of impressive finds it revealed.

He must have returned from Egypt fired with enthusiasm by what he has witnessed. With a mysterious ancient site virtually in his own back yard, it was only a matter of weeks before he ordered the excavations at Camelot Moat and virtually no time at all, before they began.

For reasons which remain inexplicable to everyone, Sassoon's excavations were in the shape of a star, leading at least one modern local historian to speculate that his motivations for doing this may have had some occult basis.

"At the present time (June1923) extensive excavations are being made at the island formed by Camlet Moat at Trent Park Cockfosters, in the interest of historical research. The water has been drained from the moat, and many strong beams of oak, forming the basis of two drawbridges, have been found. These will be preserved. Diggings in the shape of a star are in progress." Fred Fisk, Enfield Weekly Herald 22/6/1923.

Ignoring their unusual shape for a moment, Sassoon's excavations contrasted markedly with the Bevans' amateurish dig. His were of the "no expense spared" variety. Capable help was hired. Digging proceeded fast, efficiently and on a far more extensive scale. Consequently, the dig quickly turned up a number of significant and revealing discoveries.

Full details of the drawbridge were finally revealed, for instance, in this extract of a report by The Barnet Press on a talk given to the Lyonsdown Society by by S.H. Widdicombe, author of **Barnet and its Past**.

"The drawbridge was 38ft in length, 17 feet wide on the inner side and 8ft 6inches on the outer side, the timbers were all one foot square." The Barnet Press, 23/2/24.

It wasn't just large. It was massive.

Moreover, flint walls were found, resembling those of a Castle. One part of a wall was constructed of *"huge pieces of stone"* similar to the remains of a megalithic monument. Another was built from chunks of flint *"as big as a man's head."*

In places, the wall was *"five and a half feet thick."* This was clearly not the usual, low status dwelling associated with the average moated house or homestead.

This looked, to all intents and purposes, like a miniature castle. And either, the Humphrey de Bohun who had fortified his Manor here in 1347 had made an exceptionally good job of it, or these substantial il foundations had remained from an earlier time, possibly de Mandeville's or even before.

Illustration 6: Sir Phillip Sassoon, the last private owner of Trent Park, where Camelot Moat is located.

The Enfield Weekly Herald tells us: *"It is thought by the owner, Sir Phillip Sassoon, that this was the foundation of a castle at which Sir Geoffrey de Mandeville resided, the present moat is much larger than that of 1773. Many tiles and rubbish have been met with."*
Enfield Weekly Herald.22.6.23.

Sir Phillip may have inherited the castle theory from the Bevans. But if it sounds like a castle, looks like a castle, has a castle's drawbridge, a castle's moat, a castle's dungeon and is called a castle, what would you think it was ?

According to the current information board (2009) erected at the moat by the local council, it's a small thatched dwelling of no special interest. Clearly they commissioned someone who doesn't do research. Meanwhile back at the excavations, let's take a look at the full description of the unearthed walls.

"Already, a massive wall, two feet below the surface and going down to a depth of eight feet, has been met with, the clay has been cleared from one side. One part of the wall is constructed of huge pieces of stone. Further on a section is of flints as large as a man's head. A third section is constructed of beautiful tiles three quarters of an inch thick. The length of the wall, which in some parts, is about five and a half feet thick, unearthed so far, is about forty feet. "

S.H. Widdicombe's report in February the following year tells us that the excavation progressed and by then;

"74 feet of the walls of the old Manor House had been found about five feet below the surface of the ground."

The sheer size of the walls, together with the description of their beautiful tiling, suggests an impressive residence of some quality. A place fit for an Earl, or even a King ? But what of any other finds ? What do they suggest?

Well, to be honest, there aren't many more, apart from the Roman shoes, Roman dagger and some ancient horse shoes *"of quaint pattern."*

These items were put on display at Mr. Widdicombe's lecture to The Lyonsdown Society in Barnet on Feb 12th, 1924. No-one knows where they are today.

The fact that so few smaller finds were discovered raises a question about the "rubbish" that was mentioned earlier. One man's rubbish is another's treasure. "Rubbish" is gold dust to a modern archaeologist. You never know what you will discover amongst it and the smallest fragments can be extremely informative.

In some ways it is a disappointment that no other significant finds were unearthed because it adds little to our understanding of the site and its history. Nevertheless, Sir Phillip's excavations proved one very important fact, beyond a shadow of a doubt:

That the property on Camelot Moat was a substantial building, with walls and a hefty drawbridge commensurate with a small castle or fortified manor house.

The only other subject worthy of note in any of the articles or reports was the rumour of the treasure in the well.

Illustrations 7: The north side of Camelot Moat.

CHAPTER SIX

THE TREASURE
IN THE WELL

The notion that there is treasure hidden down the well seems firmly attached to all legends of Camelot Moat.

The Bevans' version of the tale suggested that the treasure belonged to Sir Geoffrey de Mandeville who was anxious to prevent it falling into the wrong hands during the War of the Roses. S.H. Widdicombe's version of the tale, recounted during a lecture about Sir Phillip Sassoon's excavations was simply:

"The well is said to have a paved bottom, under which there is buried a large chest containing gold and precious stones."

He adds the interesting footnote that: *"The treasure is guarded by the ghost of Geoffrey de Mandeville and nobody is able to approach it."*

He also includes an explanation for the ghost's presence;

" Geoffrey de Mandeville was attained for high treason during 1144. When in hiding, according to an old legend, he fell into a well near the moat and was drowned."

The earliest documented mention of this treasure dates from 1773 when a Mr Ford undertook a survey of the site.

"At the north east corner is a deep well, paved at the bottom, in which it is pretended lies an iron chest, which cannot be drawn up to the top, and that the last owner to whom the chase belonged, being attained of high treason, hid himself in a hollow tree and falling into this well, perished miserably."

The first place I came across the story was in **Volume I** of **Village London** by Edward Walford M.A. from where the above extract is taken.

If this tale has been passed by word of mouth from generation to generation, since the time of de Mandeville, nearly nine hundred years ago, there may be an element of truth in it somewhere, but where ?

The consistent elements connected to this legend are that the treasure belongs to de Mandeville, it is at the bottom of the well and de Mandeville died by falling into the well.

The first thing to dismiss is the manner of Geoffrey de Mandeville's death. The idea that he drowned falling into a well is a complete fabrication. Sir Geoffrey de Mandeville did die in 1144, but not at Camelot Moat. In August of that year, it is recorded that he received an arrow wound to the head at the siege of Burwell Castle. He died the following month at Mildenhall in Suffolk as a direct result of the wound.

That doesn't mean it wasn't his treasure. There's actually a strong possibility he may have amassed great wealth in goods and chattels from his opportunistic career change to archetypal "robber baron" during the ruinously anarchistic period of the 1140s when Stephen and Matilda vied for the crown.

De Mandeville switched sides shamelessly, depending on who was offering the most attractive rewards and as robber barons go, he was, by all accounts, the worst.

In an age marked by treachery and brutality, he managed to excel in both, earning himself a reputation as: *"the devil in human form"*.

By 1143, he had double-crossed Matilda, betrayed Stephen and was outlawed. This was when his career as a robber baron really took off. Seizing the opportunity to profit from the in-fighting for the crown, he gathered an army of mercenaries, including William de Say (his brother-in-law) and the Earl of Norfolk, then set out to inflict an unwarranted reign of terror on the Fenlands.

He seized Ely, sacked Ramsey Abbey, evicted or killed the monks and looted any valuables he could get his hands on. Making Ramsey his headquarters, he ransacked and looted more towns, including Cambridge, until his bloodthirsty career was brought to an end, as we have heard, by the arrow of an archer defending Burwell Castle.

During this period, he would have acquired many chests full of other people's gold, silver, jewellery, precious stones and other valuables.

The treasure of Camelot Moat, therefore, could easily have been a part of de Mandeville's loot. If it exists, or existed, where is it today? Well, the one place it probably isn't is down the well.

These days, the well is no longer a sturdy brick-lined construction with a tiled floor. It is a muddy crater in the north east corner of the moat's island and has been well and truly dug out, by someone obviously in search of the legendary treasure. But who?

According to Ford's survey in 1773, the paved floor at the bottom of the well was still intact at that time and it remained that way until the Bevans' excavations.

Nesta Bevan openly admitted, with some disappointment, that with the death of Robert Bevan, the family's previous enthusiasm for the excavations ceased, leaving the treasure as yet undiscovered, so I think we can safely rule them out.

That leaves Sir Phillip Sassoon as the likely candidate.

Yet if Sir Phillip had found anything, I am sure we would have heard about it. He seemed the sort of flamboyant personality that would have revelled in the publicity spotlight resulting from such a discovery.

He was also rich enough in his own right not to be too bothered about finding 'treasure' for its monetary worth. It would have been peanuts compared to his own personal wealth. No, he was in the hunt for the excitement, fame and glory.

Unfortunately, there are no records specifically relating to the well, or anything being found in it, so we have no idea whether he dug down and found the tiled well floor, or removed it to enable his men to dig deeper in search of De Mandeville's loot. Or indeed whether the tiled floor or the treasure is still there lurking deep beneath the mud and clay.

Then again, maybe there was no treasure to find.

Or perhaps it was a different kind of treasure, altogether?

Illustrations 8: The the remains of the well in the north east corner of Camelot Moat.

CHAPTER SEVEN

A PLACE OF INITIATION

Often, tales of treasure at ancient sites, usually a sacred site, are allegorical and are said to indicate that the place holds some kind of hidden knowledge, or wisdom, or power, which is the true treasure and may be released as an insight to those who seek it.

This could mean it is a place with some kind of arcane knowledge literally built into it, like Rosslyn Chapel or Glastonbury Abbey, or that it's an oracular shrine, a place of vision, a place of inspiration, a place with healing powers, a place somehow encoded with the secrets of an ancient mystery tradition, or a place that holds some other knowledge, arcane or otherwise.
It could even relate to a place of initiation into the mysteries.

This brings us back to Camelot Moat's tale of treasure, because its 'drowned-down-the-well' theme, sounds very like a symbolic death as part of an initiation ritual. One version of the legend even adds some extra detail which points towards this possibility.

This version claims that De Mandeville, was on the run from the King's men (presumably King Stephen) who wanted to arrest him for treason. It was the night of the full moon and he hid in a hollow oak on the moat. At midnight, he ventured out and fell to his death in the well.

The extra elements of specific interest are: the fact that the hollow tree was an oak, the time De Mandeville fell to his death was midnight and that it all happened by the light of a full moon.

A druid's oak, the witching hour and a bright full moon, traditionally a time for unorthodox ceremony, are an extremely mystical combination and suggest a ritual.

The added element of a completely fabricated death suggests what the ritual was; an initiation, probably into a mystery tradition.

Initiations in shamanic, pagan, masonic and druidic traditions can all incorporate a symbolic death, or near-death experience, so that the initiate is symbolically re-born into a new phase of life with a new understanding provided by a personal insight into life-after-death.

The Christian baptism may be a remnant of an initiation by water. People who have experienced a near-death by drowning often report that "their whole lives flashed before them." Maybe that was the whole point of the baptism; to experience the reality of life-after-death by undergoing a near drowning, rather than the gentle soaking a baptism entails these days.

Do any other wells provide evidence they could have been used for an initiation by water ?

As far as I know, there is only one. The Chalice Well in Glastonbury. There it is believed that a stone-lined chamber beneath the well-head was probably used for under-water initiation rituals. How interesting that it is located in Avalon, an area at the heart of the Arthurian Grail Mysteries.

Is that another clue to the nature of the mystery tradition located here at Camelot Moat, or is it yet another Arthurian synchronicity ?

Curiously, there is another well, not too far from Camelot Moat, whose name suggests it could have been an extremely important ancient sacred place and a possible location for some very specific ritual practices.

It's marked on old Ordnance Survey Maps as Nodens' (or Noddins) Well and was located on the western side of the mansion, on the edge of the woods, close to where a modern-looking house has been built.

There is no sign of a well here, today, but there are six manhole
t

manhole covers in the vicinity, one of which could conceal the exact spot where the well was capped off.

It is a great pity the location of Nodens' Well has been lost since the name alone tells us it would have been of great significance.

The Great God Nodens was a Celtic British deity with an associationto healing, so it is probable that this may have been a healing well of immense antiquity.

He is a complex deity with many facets to his character. We're reliably informed that he combines the qualities of a hunting god with attributes comparable to the Roman Mars, Mercury and Silvanus (a woodland deity). In the Celtic pantheons, he's connected to Lugh, the Celtic sun God, but I believe his closest associations are with the Irish mythological figure Nuada of the Silver Hand and the Welsh Gwyn ap Nudd, a god of the underworld, who is said to reside under Glastonbury Tor (which, coincidentally, overlooks the Chalice Well mentioned earlier).

Through his connection to the underworld, Nodens is a God of dreams and sleep. The terms "nodding off" and "The Land of Nod" may derive from his name.

In ancient Britain, his most famous place of worship was a temple complex at Lydney in Gloucestershire, perched high atop a hill within the ramparts of an earlier iron-age hill fort.

The design of the temple suggests it was a place where pilgrims would come to sleep, but not just to rest, this was ritual sleep at an oracular shrine. Nodens' temples were dream incubation centres, where pilgrims hoped that their nocturnal slumbers would bring them a divine vision, a dream of healing, or of divine guidance for their lives.

Sites with this ancient dedication are extremely rare, exceptionally important and in urgent need of preservation.

To have a Nodens Well in Trent Park suggests it could have

been a very important site of exceptional antiquity and deserving of further investigation.

As a Romano-British deity, a shrine to Nodens would possibly explain the small roman finds that turned up in the excavations nearby at Camelot Moat, as well as supporting the previously mentioned notion that the name Camelot in this area, has definite Celtic origins.

More importantly, if Nodens had a sacred, healing well here, somewhere nearby there may also be the undiscovered remains of one of his dream incubation temples.

Who knows, a temple could even have been located on the hill above Nodens Well.

That could be Camelot Hill, the site of Camelot Moat.

Illustration 9:
A statue, possibly of the Romano-Celtic deity Nodens, found in a well beneath Southwark Cathedral and now on display in a corridor outside the Cathedral refectory.

CHAPTER EIGHT

IS CAMELOT MOAT
A SACRED SITE ?

Whether it was a sacred site in the past is debatable. These days, there is no doubt about it. Camelot moat is definitely regarded, rightly or wrongly, as a sacred site by a great many of its visitors. The well in the north east corner of the isle, in particular, is a focus for this belief and is considered to be a holy well, even though it now resembles nothing more than a mere muddy hole.

A beech next to the well is quite obviously venerated as a "Clootie Tree" or "Rag Tree." Its branches are festooned with lengths of cloth, ribbon and other multi-coloured offerings.

Tradition has it that you soak a piece of cloth in the water of the well or spring and then tie it to a branch of the rag tree while saying a prayer or blessing to the Genius Loci, the spirit of place, who can take the form of a pre-Christian goddess, a local nature spirit, or if the well is in close proximity to a church, a Saint.

There are many examples around the country. At Madron in Cornwall a Rag Tree stands beside the well and the ruined chapel. At St. Kenelm's, Romsley, in the Clent Hills, a Clootie Tree marks the Holy Spring. At the Swallowhead Spring near Silbury Hill in Wiltshire, many of the trees nearby have been decorated with a veritable rainbow of offerings.

It's an ancient practice, usually done to seek healing or simply to honour the spirit of the well or spring. In either case, it is a continuation of the ancient Celtic tradition of making votive offerings to a goddess of the sacred waters whether they be wells, springs, ponds, rivers or lakes. Holy wells and springs mark some of the most ancient sacred sites in Great Britain. There are numerous Bride's Wells, Mary Wells, St. Anne's Wells and Lady Wells throughout Britain, some only surviving as a place name rather than an actual water source.

Does this make Camelot Moat a sacred place?

Actually, it does. A sacred site is anywhere that a number of people regard as significant or special for spiritual or religious reasons.

I personally believe that the moat may have been, in the remote past, some kind of sacred enclosure and that the well was the focus for an oracular shrine. I can present no evidence for this claim other than the psychic impressions I have picked up from the place itself.

These included the notion that the well was originally in the care of a small group of women and that it was linked to Monken Hadley by a ceremonial or processional route that is now marked by Camlet Way.

That is only my subjective opinion, rightly or wrongly.

The local council definitely do not regard it as a place of any sanctity. In 2004, they ordered the Rag Tree to be felled as they considered it to be leaning at a dangerous angle and were worried it might fall on someone who would sue them.

This excuse was patently nonsense since the tree was firmly leaning on, and supported by, another tree, so there was actually no chance whatsoever of it falling on anyone, but that didn't dissuade them from sending a couple of tree surgeons to deal with it just in case.

As things turned out, local protesters also turned up and prevented the tree from being completely destroyed. Instead the upper part of the tree was felled leaving the lower branches to remain available for offerings.

This sad affair gave the impression that someone at Enfield Council wants to discourage the use of Camlet Moat as a sacred site. The notice boards at the moat reinforce this opinion. They make no reference to any possible sacred or mystical significance.

In fact they attempt to misguide visitors by presenting it as a simple "homestead" moat of little significance. Here's what the information board at one entrance says:

"Spread across the Mediaeval landscape were thousands of modest rural moated sites of which Camlet is a fine and well-preserved example. Sites like these are some way down the social scale from castles and big manor houses and as they tend visually to be relatively modest is was only in the 1960s that archaeologists realised that they formed a distinct class of field monuments in their own right. Since then it has been shown they survive in remarkably large numbers with well-over 5,000 having already been identified in England and with new discoveries being made every year. Most date from 1150 – 1500 A.D. approx.
They vary in size and complexity usually comprising a central platform – rectangular in form, on which was a domestic house often with outbuildings and garden, partly or completely surrounded by a moat with a flat-bottomed ditch. This could be crossed by bridges, as at Camlet. Excavated timber thought to be from a bridge was dated using dendrochronology, or tree-ring-dating, to 1357."

It is illustrated by a picture of a suitably modest thatched building with a simple wooden footbridge over the moat.

No mention of castle-like, five-feet-thick flint walls, forty feet long, ornately tiled in sections. No mention of subterranean dungeons, a drawbridge of impressive proportions, or finds from the Roman period.

The information board at the other entrance is just as misleading and riddled with errors.

"Nothing is known of the origins of Camlet Moat, but it must have come into existence in some form when Enfield Chase was created as a hunting preserve around 1140. The first probable occupant was Richard Pounz, Keeper of the Chase in the 1320s. In 1426, the lodge was demolished. Poor quality excavations in the late 1880's and again in 1923 suggest the lodge was quite substantial with rubble masonry walls and glazed tiled floors in some rooms. The name Camelot

remains a mystery. It first appears in local rec
piece of the drawbridge's frame has been rec
cally dated to c 1357."

There is also an illustration of the dr

"Drawing of the framework thou
drawbridge over the moat, removed from the mo
ily in 1923."

No mention here of the otherwise notorious Sir Geoffrey De Mandeville despite the fact that The Domesday book records:

"At Enfield mention is made of a park belonging to Geoffrey de Mandeville."

Instead we are told its first owner was an unremarkable chap, Richard Pounz. In fact Richard Pounz was granted the title of Keeper of The Chase by one of the Humphrey de Bohuns (who also doesn't get a mention), probably the one who fortified the Manor House here and built the mighty drawbridge.

Other errors include the date of the demolition. 1439 according to the respected local historian, David Pam, not 1426. Nor were the 1923 excavations by the Bevan family (who were responsible for the earlier 1880's dig) but by Sir Phillip Sassoon who owned the Park from 1912, having inherited it from his father, Sir Edward Sassoon, who had purchased it in 1903.

But enough of this petty griping. Whether Camelot moat's misinformation boards mention it or not, a large number of people regard the place as special, significant or sacred. The question we need to ask next is; why?

The answer might surprise you. Because, although Cockfosters' secret Camelot is not widely or officially acknowledged as a sacred site, it actually has something in common with many of the world's great spiritual centres and places of pilgrimage, including Lourdes, Fatima, Knock and Walsingham.

46

CHAPTER NINE

OUR LADY OF CAMELOT

It's not just the well that indicates that visitors to the moat regard it as a place of sanctity. All around the isle you'll see shrines at the base of trees, some of them created by people with obvious artistic ability. In one of the excavation ditches, for instance, there's currently (2009) a very nice installation created from interwoven twigs which form a protective U-shaped shelter around a central wooden block or altar, upon which stands a white statue that appears to be the Goddess Athena, but also bears a passing resemblance to Britannia.

The most conspicuous creations though are a number of bender shelters, inside which are shrines, crystals, lanterns, dream-catchers, logs to sit on and all kinds of other interesting magical bits and bobs.

Although created by specific individuals, these places seem to be frequently used by anyone who comes to the moat. They provide somewhere to sit and enjoy the peace and tranquillity of this secluded woodland location.

Reasons for coming here vary enormously. Some people come specifically to meditate and seek inspiration, or spiritual guidance. Clearly there is something in the nature of the place that leads them to believe some kind of divine interaction or inspiration is possible here.

To others, it is a place of healing, for those who seek respite from some physical ailment or affliction. By the look of the stagnant sludge in the well, I would imagine drinking the water from here would have the opposite effect, so its not a place to "take the waters" but there is definitely a sense of a "healing" power in the general atmosphere of the place and at some specific places around the isle.

Others, particularly on warm summer weekends, flock here out of sheer curiosity, having been told about the moat by friends.

They take great delight in touring the shrines, with dogs and gaggles of children, seeing what curiosities have been hung from the trees and speculating on what strange goings-on must occur here by the light of the witch's full moon.

Unless it's a busy summer weekend, most visitors to the moat will have the place to themselves. The only occasions when there will be anything resembling a crowd, is when one of the groups who use the site turn up for a ceremony or outing.

These could include one of the local Druid groves, or the very nice local witchy ladies, who occasionally hold ceremonies here on one of the eight natural festivals of the year; the winter or summer solstices, the spring or autumn equinoxes, or one of the four Celtic fire festivals, Candlemass (Ist February), Beltain (Mayday), Lammas (August Ist) or Halloween (October 31st).

Other spiritual groups use the site for a variety of reasons, including the followers of a Holy Man from Southern India called Atmachaitanya, who first came here in the eighties following a vision. The place, he said, had called to him from the other side of the world and so he came here with a group of his followers, some of whom live in London, to bless it with traditional Sanskrit chants and to perform a short ceremony.

He also said that, in his vision, one of the trees there bore a Sanskrit OM symbol on its trunk. It was found in a tree on the north side of the well, but has since grown out and is now virtually unrecognisable.

The notes I made at the time include his comment that there were huge stones beneath the ground here. I don't think he had read the Enfield Archeaological Society reports that would support this (neither had I at the time), so his intuitive insight was accurate. He also said it was a place of great spiritual power, but not yet recognised as such!

Other groups include a drumming circle, an Earth Healing group, dowsing groups investigating "ley" alignments and a paranormal investigation society who, I am told, turn up every Halloween, in the hope of catching an annual visitation of Sir Geoffrey de Mandeville's ghost who is said to appear on the most haunted night of the year.

In contrast to all this mystical stuff are the practical and down-to-earth Ground Force volunteers who have been looking after the moat for some years, repairing fences, dredging the sludge from the moat, clearing undergrowth and generally making themselves useful and keeping the place tidy.

There's also at least one bunch who seem to just turn up to light a fire, drink beer and then leave all their cans and other mess behind. It takes all sorts.

Most visitors to the moat, by and large, just come to experience the atmosphere and presence of the place.

A significant number, though, come in the hope of witnessing a very specific presence here; a "White Lady" apparition, similar to reported sightings of The Virgin Mary.

Many people have seen her, including myself. In fact, I was the first person to publicly mention this phenomenon in my books **Earthstars** (1990), **Earthstars The Visionary Landscape** (2000) and in several magazine articles.

According to one of the park rangers, dog walkers have seen her drifting wispily across the path near the moat. Visitors to the moated isle have told me they have seen her floating between the trees, particularly in the vicinity of the well.

What they normally describe is a radiant, ethereal image of a woman who appears to be wearing a long white gown with some kind of tie around the waist and a head covering, like a veil, scarf or headdress. Most often, her arms are open and outstretched beside her, in a classic welcoming gesture frequently seen in images of The Virgin Mary.

Understandably, one or two witnesses have assumed this was a ghost and were suitably alarmed by their brief encounter.

Many others, mostly those who could be a little bit psychic, or spiritually inclined, said that what they felt was as important as what they saw, because the apparition radiated an emotional charge.

It was a feeling of love, goodness and affection. It was intense. A feeling that they were in the presence of some great beneficent, caring spiritual being. That was my experience, too, on the first occasion I saw her and, I have to say, it came as quite a shock.

Mostly, her apparition would be fleeting and of human proportions but on my first visit to the moat, she appeared larger, as a huge radiant presence towering over the moat's tree line, her height maybe 50 to 60 feet (this is described more fully in **Earthstars The Visionary Landscape**). And of course, it was not something solid or material. She was more like an effect of the light or of energy.

I entered the woods beneath this giant presence, and could no longer see it, but I could still sense her energy. Then, when I crossed to the moat's isle, there was a remarkable and immediate change in the atmosphere. It became so intense, it literally made the hair on the back of my neck stand on end.

On that first occasion I couldn't stay on the moat for very long. It made me disorientated and dizzy. Over twenty years have passed since then and in all that time I have never felt the energy of the place so strongly, nor seen the White Lady in quite the same way. In fact, over the years, her appearance has varied quite markedly.

Once she manifested as a mediaeval Guinevere look-alike, complete with conical hat, hung with a veil. At least that's what it appeared to be at first. When her head turned, it was clear the distinctive hat had two points not one. I've met at least one other person has seen her as Guinevere, though given the Camelot connection, I'm amazed there aren't more.

Another time, she appeared to be wearing a crescent-moon head

-dress and bore more than a passing resemblance to the image on card number two of the Tarot Major Arcana, The High Priestess, who is the Keeper of the ancient Mysteries, an extremely significant card since this place seems to have more than its fair share of local mysteries as well as more than a passing association with the greater mysteries of The Holy Grail.

The White Lady's most common manifestation bore a noticeable resemblance to a typical image of The Virgin Mary.

Because I had seen her take other forms, I didn't automatically assume that this was a visitation of the BVM, 'Blessed Virgin Mary' although I knew that others might.

Also I knew, from my subsequent research into the phenomena, that even Bernadette Soubirou didn't at first think her vision's at Lourdes were The Virgin Mary, either.

Until Bernadette spoke to the local Parish priest, she simply called her the " White Lady." It seems to have been the priest who put everything into a good Catholic context and told her that the "White Lady" was the Mary the Divine Mother.

It's highly likely that the phenomena is actually something that may pre-date our Christian culture and be open to broader interpretation.

Most interestingly, bearing in mind our starting point for all this was a place called Camelot, is the possibility that 'The White Lady' apparition has strong connections to the legends of the Holy Grail. In fact, she may be a representation of the Grail Maiden.

There is an anonymous addition to Chretien de Troyes **Perceval**, which contains material that supports this idea and throws much light on the subject.

It is called **The Elucidation** and its author, whoever he was, deemed it important enough to add it to Chretien's work as a prologue, rather than an afterthought.

In my opinion, it is an extremely important piece since it may express the true nature of the Grail far more clearly than any other of the romances.

The Elucidation explains, not only how The Grail was originally held by "The Maidens of the Holy Wells," but how it was lost, and how Logres subsequently became a barren and desolate land. The subsequent search for the Grail, ordered by Arthur, was a quest for the one thing that could bring about the redemption of the wasteland.

The essential story is that long ago, before the reign of King Arthur, the land was blessed with great abundance and fertility. This was due, in the main, to the enchantment of the Maidens of the Wells, who possessed, and were keepers of, the Grail.

Throughout the realm, every sacred well or spring, had a guardian who was a Grail Maiden. To every passing traveller or visitor, she offered the sacred waters in a golden cup.

Indeed, some say that these were the very waters of life and inspiration, offering far more than thirst-quenching refreshment.

As guardians of the wells and springs, and the voice of the sacred waters, the maidens themselves may not actually have been corporeal, but otherworldly spirits of place. The tale does not actually say. In those days, these distinctions were probably understood and did not need to be spelled out bluntly

Under the aegis of the Grail Maidens, all was well, the land was fertile and the people content. Then along came King Amangon, a lecherous, greedy lout who, so the story tells us, raped one of the well maidens, stole her sacred golden cup, carried her off and enslaved her as a serving wench.

> *" Ill luck was to come of it,*
> *For no maiden served again*
> *Or came forth from that well*

To help any man who happened by
And requested sustenance there."

The life-giving sacred waters dried up. The voice of the well was never heard again. Its guardian never seen again.

Rather than learn from the dire results of King Amangon's actions, his men followed his example, raping other Grail Maidens and stealing their magic golden cups.

In response to these violations, the Maidens of the Wells withdrew themselves and their magical guardianship from the world. The wells dried up, and the regenerative powers of the land were lost, leaving it barren and devoid of enchantment.

> *"Never afterwards did any maiden serve*
> *Or come forth from any of the wells;*
> *Know that this is the truth.*
> *My lords, in this way*
> *The land went into decline*
> *And the king who had so wronged them*
> *And those who'd followed his example*
> *All met a dreadful end.*
> *The land was so wasted*
> *That no tree ever bloomed there again,*
> *The grasses and flowers withered,*
> *And the streams dried up.*
> *Afterwards no one could locate*
> *The court of the Rich Fisher. "*

The fact that **The Elucidation** describes the Grail Maidens as being "in the wells" as well as "of the wells" strengthens the possibility that they are an allegory for the spirit of the land, who some of our ancestors must have actually seen as an apparition of a Goddess figure at her well or spring.

Every Grail Maiden is strongly connected to the numinous qualities of her sacred well or spring and in total control of the waters of life in its broadest sense, as the generative life force within nature as well as the power of the Holy Waters. She controls these powers and properties absolutely and is able to bestow them freely upon the worthy, or withdraw them from the undeserving as she sees fit.

It is highly likely, given the content of **The Elucidation**, that her origins lie in pre-Christian traditions which were re-worked to form the basis of the Grail Romances and the foundation of the secret Goddess tradition within Arthurian Legend.

My personal belief is that she represents an ancient Goddess figure who once was seen to manifest as a local spirit of place over a wide enough area for her to be considered a Goddess of the land or of the Earth.

She is also "The Lady" that the knights serve and pledge allegiance to. As Lewis Spence points out in **The Mysteries of Britain**;

"The whole legend of the Grail, although diverted to Christian uses, is indeed entirely derived from sources which may be described as Druidical."

The tendency to comprehend these apparitions in modern times as visitations of The Virgin Mary, is a direct result of the time, place, culture and the beliefs of the observer.

To me, with my multi-faith interests, mystical inclinations and Gnostic tendencies, she was Robert Grave's "White Goddess" the British Goddess Bride, The Tarot High Priestess, Guinevere and a whole mixture of other divine female archetypes, as well as Mary, the Divine Mother (we are of course, talking here in terms of archetypal principles, not a human individual).

I could easily understand how an ancient Roman might regard a similar apparition as the Goddess Diana, or Venus. How, to an ancient Greek, she might be a visitation of Artemis or Aphrodite. To an Egyptian, Isis. As Dion Fortune once said,

"All goddesses are one goddess, just as all Gods are one God."

The one thing that was consistent, even when she was simply sensed rather than seen, was the presence and emotion she radiated. It was an overwhelming feeling of love, kindness and affection. It was intense. A feeling that you were in the presence of some great beneficent spiritual being.

By whatever name she may have been known as an ancient Goddess (and there were probably many) she is clearly related to the White Goddess who was Robert Graves' muse and who formed the subject of his famous book. She is also the feminine principle known as "The Inspirer" in druidic tradition.

She may even have appeared at the moat as a being of pure energy. Many photographs taken there show mysterious blobs of white light or some energy presence which was not immediately apparent to the normal senses when the photograph was taken.

One example was taken by myself in normal day light. When processed and printed (this was in the days of film rather than digital cameras) the shot showed several oval light shapes that look as if they are flying by. The remaining shots on the film were perfectly normal.

Other photographs taken by another regular visitor to the moat show mysterious orbs of light. In one instance they seem to be bubbling up out of the well and in another, they appear to be rising from the ground in the ceremonial circle used by the druids and other groups.

The most spectacular shots were sent to me anonymously and show a glowing mass of white light vaguely shaped like a human figure, distinctly reminiscent of the "White Lady" image.

Whether these are genuine photographs or some kind of artificially created image, I do not know. All I can say is they certainly bear a blurry resemblance to the apparitions I saw.

Whatever the explanation for these 'White Lady' apparitions, if they resemble The Elucidations' Grail Maidens of the wells, they are strikingly appropriate to a place called Camelot.

Our Lady of Camelot Moat, could actually be one of the Grail Maidens of the Wells..

As such she is part of a phenomenon that lies at the root of the mysteries of The Holy Grail.

So our Camelot, whether it has any verifiable historical Arthurian connections or not, certainly has some astonishing connections to the legends of The Holy Grail.

Illustration 11:
A strange blob of energy photographed at Camelot Moat and resembling the "White Lady' apparitions frequently seen there.

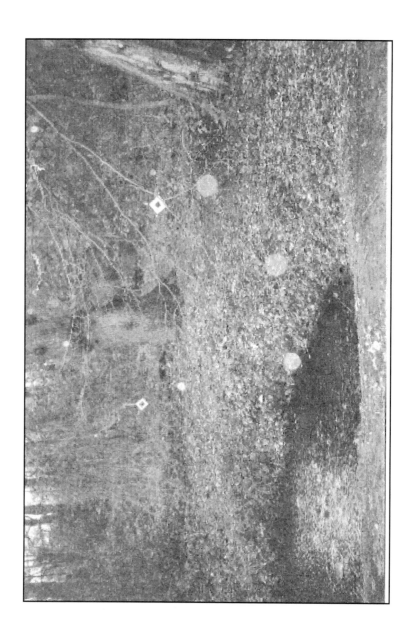

Illustration 12:
Mysterious light orbs that appear to be bubbling out of the holy well (view on side).

Illustration 13: More light orbs at one of the moat's tree shrines.

Illustration 14: More light orbs captured on camera at Camelot Moat, some oval, looking as if they are flying by.

Illustration 15: The Virgin Mary in the pose she's most often seen in at Camelot Moat.

Illustration 16: Apparition of The Virgin Mary at Fatima.

CHAPTER TEN

LEY LINES, EARTHSTARS
AND THE ROUND TABLE.

If the White Lady of the well is an aspect of the Goddess of the Land and a guardian or controller of its vital forces and their flow, the mysterious subject of Leys and Earth energies ought also to play a part in this, since they are thought to be conduits of the same vital, animating current within the landscape.

Predictably, they do.

Not only is Camelot Moat a focal point for numerous straight forward (if there is such a thing) ley alignments, it occupies a key position in a number of quite remarkable geometric patterns on the London landscape, defined principally by other ancient sacred sites, hilltops, old Parish churches and so on.

Like apparitions of the Virgin Mary, the subject of leys and mysterious Earth Energies are huge, dinosaur-sized bones of contention, usually cast into the pit of non-existent nuttiness by the world of serious academia.

By contrast, they are grasped and embraced eagerly by the more mystically inclined and those whose beliefs in these matters are built upon a more intuitive understanding.

They are not, shall we say, subjects where there are clear-cut and proven definitions and theories backed up by stacks of statistical evidence.

My personal opinions on the subject include the conviction that they can be used as paths of enlightenment by anyone who is inclined to investigate the phenomena.

Leys and associated alignments are principally defined by ancient sacred sites, places of ritual, places where our mundane world is overlapped by the spiritual realms.

These are places that our ancestors credited with otherwordly, magical properties and powers; where the ancient gods (and goddesses) were seen; places of power, vision, inspiration or healing; entrances to the spirit world.

In my opinion, they still are.

Hardly surprising then that we find odd, inexplicable things happening at, or associated with, some of these sites.

Leys fall into two types. The most contentious being energy leys, because the only evidence for them is subjective, usually just the opinion of a dowser with a twig, pendulum or a pair of L-shaped dowsing rods.

To add to the confusion, energy leys, can be overground or underground. Underground lines are likely to be meandering serpentine currents like the dragon lines of Feng Shui. Overground lines are more likely to be straight.

Sadly, neither are likely to have any objective evidence for their existence. It's a belief thing. Unless you're a good dowser. Then it is down to personal experience and practice.

Last time I tried to dowse energy currents at Camelot Moat, I gave up. As I walked around the moat I picked up so many lines radiating out from it, I lost count. The bent angle rods I was using flapped backwards and forwards like windscreen wipers in a hurricane.

The moat is either a very powerful hub for these energies or I am a duff dowser. Quite frankly, it doesn't matter which of these you choose to believe as I suspect that both contain an element of truth.

Let's move on to the second type of ley, one that is clearly marked by a verifiable linear alignment of sites. Camelot has at least two of these.

1: The Beltaine sunrise line.

Camlet Moat lines up through the Trent Park Obelisk (you'll see it if you go there), along the length of The Meadway in Barnet, through Whiting's Hill and on to St. John's Church Stanmore. This is not strictly a ley, though it is a Beltaine (Mayday) sunrise alignment. Various versions of the Bel name relate to ancient sun gods. Beli Mawr, Baal, Belenus, etc, so the fact that it's a sunrise line may be significant. I have a feeling that Whiting's Hill may have originally been a "Bell's Hill" a site dedicated to one of the old sun-gods and where Beltaine rites were anciently celebrated. I base this assumption purely on an intuitive hunch and the fact that Bell's Hill Road leads to it. This flimsy evidence is compounded by the fact that May's Lane also leads towards it. Beltaine is celebrated on the eve of the first day of May.

2: Camelot's St. Mary's line.

Camlet moat also aligns to the small, hilltop Mother Church of Barnet, The Parish Church of St. Mary the Virgin in Church Hill, East Barnet. This is another spot where I have experienced apparitions of a goddess or Marian figure. It also has a well that is now covered over, though springs do leak out of the churchyard at certain times of year. The alignment continues from here through to St. James' Church in Friern Barnet, on to the remains of a venerable oak known as Dick Turpin's Oak (now just a stump) beside the North Circular Road near the Vue Cinema/Hollywood bowl complex on Finchley High Rd. It can be extended further to the chapel of Fortune Green cemetery in West Hampstead and even further to the Parish Church of Barnes, another very old St. Mary's.

These simple leys are nothing compared to the geometric patterns Camelot Moat is implicated in - an entire network of intricate sacred geometry which covers the whole of Greater London and connects to other similar ancient sites the length and breadth of the land. A sort of spiritual national grid.

The first and most obvious design is what I call The Barnet Triangle, an almost perfect equilateral triangle on the landscape formed by Camelot Moat, St. Mary the Virgin Monken Hadley and St. Mary the Virgin, East Barnet, the oldest church in the area.

One side of the triangle is formed by the alignment between Camelot Moat and St, Mary's East Barnet.

From this simple triangle, the geometry becomes a little more complex linking to a vast and beautiful network of inter-related designs: including circles, hexagrams, pentagrams, decagons, enneagrams, heptagrams, an eight-pointed star and, at their most complex, twenty and thirty-point star patterns.

None are isolated individual patterns. Every single one of them interconnects with the rest to form a complex yet composite design of great significance.

The basis of the complete pattern is a recognisable groundplan of sacred geometry which has consistently been used in the design of temples, over a period of several millenia.

Remarkably, the earliest example of its use in Britain is at Stonehenge, where this geometry dictated the layout of the monument's megaliths over 3,500 years ago.

The patterns are identical. Only the scale is different. London's temple is precisely 792 times bigger than the sarsen trilithon circle at Stonehenge. That's a figure with a natural harmonic resonance to the planet built into it. 7920 is the mean diameter of the Earth in miles.

Many of London's most ancient and well-known sacred sites are mark points in this vast temple concealed within the London landscape. They include Westminster Abbey, St. Paul's Cathedral, The Tower of London, Barking Abbey, many of London's sacred hills and large number of its local Parish Churches.

It's astonishing to think they have been placed on the landscape in the same pattern as the sarsens and bluestones of Britain's most recognisable megalithic monument.

To give you some idea of the complexity and scale of this landscape temple, several of the maps and illustrations of the geometry are included here.

For a full explanation of its extent and significance, you'll need a copy of one of my other books, **Earthstars**, or **Earthstars The Visionary Landscape**, both of which can be tracked down on Amazon or the www.earthstars.co.uk website.

What is of great relevance to the book at hand is that the "Earthstars" discovery came to light as a direct result of a series of visions and dreams involving a White Goddess figure, who led me to identify the first sites in the patterns. These, needless to say, included Camelot Moat. Camelot and its "White Lady" played a prominent role in initiating the Earthstars discovery.

What the Earthstars geometry may be is also very relevant to the essential nature of the White Goddess as a representative spirit of the land.

I believe the scale of it is beyond the capabilities of human endeavour. It has to be something inherently natural, encoded in the landscape.

My understanding is that these geometric patterns are fundamental to and inherent in the structure of the Earth. They represent an energy matrix of the planetary life-force, a circuit diagram of the formative forces of creation at work within nature.

The geometric patterning within nature is obvious all around us; in the hexagonal basis of snowflakes and quartz crystals; in the way the molten lava of the 'Devil's Causeway' in Northern Ireland has shattered into hexagonal blocks as it entered the north sea: in the pentagonal limbs of starfish and dog rose petals; in the Golden Mean spirals of snail's shells, sunflower seedheads and even in the spiral arms of galactic nebulae.

The nodal points of this numinous power network must have been recognised by our ancestors and used as their ritual centres. Subsequent cultures have built successively upon those same power centres so that the geometry linking them has finally become detectable in the modern world, at certain places, through the accuracy of our modern Ordnance Survey maps and the wonders of Google Earth.

The point is, though, that in these ley alignments and Earthstars geometry, we again have a phenomenon which appears to be a manifestation of the planetary life-force.

That is exactly the power controlled by the Grail Maidens of the Wells in **The Elucidation**. They are the representatives and guardians of this power.

The White Goddess, The Grail Maidens of the Wells, the energy within Leys, the Earthstars geometry and the sacred sites which define it are all related.

They are all different manifestations of the same thing; the essential life-force.

Yet again, another of Camelot's enigmas leads to a Grail connection.

Here comes another, for which I have to thank my old friend Peter Quiller Clark (author of **Merlin the Immortal** and **Merlin Awakens**) who pointed out something quite obvious that I had completely overlooked.

Peter had also discovered a circle of sacred sites and had made the observation that they could be described as a Round Table on the landscape.

Arthur's Round Table was designed as a symbol of harmony so that all who sat around it were equal. The Earthstars Round Table is also a remarkable symbol of harmony.

All of the individual patterns which combine to create its complexity (all twenty one of them), fit together with absolute, perfect geometric harmony and precision.

They are held in dynamic equilibrium. They link in the kind of beautiful complexity that only nature can create. It's a small point, but worth noting. Another is that The Round Table was not originally Arthur's.

It was part of Guinevere's dowry. The table and the Queen came as a package. Just as the Grail Maidens of the Wells and the life-force of the land were closely associated.

The parallel here with Earthstars is obvious. The Earthstars Round Table is a construction of the planetary life force, under the protection of the Goddess of the land whose Earthly representative is the Queen, Guinevere.

As you may recall, the name Guinevere could actually mean "the spirit of life".

In the Druid tradition, the term for life-force is 'nwyvre' - an old Welsh word also meaning energy and vigour. It has its counterpart in a Gaulish word, 'wouivre', meaning spirit, and this became 'vouivre' in certain parts of France. Gwen-nwyvre, would translate as "white ghost", "white spirit" or more accurately "white spirit of life" so her name may equate to the force which animates nature.

Guinevere's name may also reveal a goddess and Marian association. In old Welsh there was no v. It was an f. Gwenerfair would be pronounced much the same and mean Venus Mary.

The White Goddess, Guinevere and the life force of the land are one in the same. Or so it would seem.

It would also appear they were Christianised through an association with the Virgin Mary and the general Marian stream.

Surprisingly, that simple fact is fundamental to the understanding of the grail mysteries, which in turn underpin the secret tradition in Arthurian Legend and a sizeable chunk of druidic teaching.

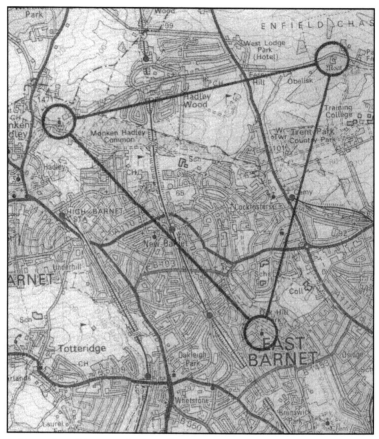

Illustration 17:
The Barnet Triangle. The top right hand point is Camelot Moat. This simple piece of geometry led to the discovery of a vast and complex series of overlaid designs linking ancient sacred sites all over London.

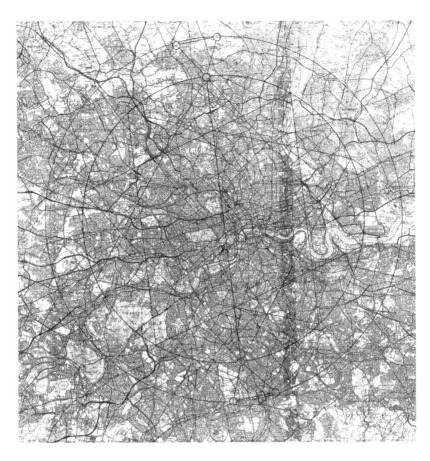

Illustration 18:
The Barnet Triangle line from Camelot Moat to St. Mary's East Barnet forms a
perfect 10-point star on the London Landscape. It's mark points clockwise from
the top are: St. Mary's East Barnet, a point in Lee Valley Park, St. Gabriel's
Wanstead Flats, a site near Maryon Park Charlton, St Dunstan's Bellingham
Green, Pollard's Hill Norbury, Caesar's Camp on Wimbkledon Common, a
mound in the grounds of Sion House Brentford, Horsendon Hill Greenford, Hill
in Watling Park, burnt Oak.

Illustration 19:
The Barnet Triangle line from St. Mary's Monken hadley to St. Mary's East Barnet forms a perfect 8 -point star on the London Landscape.

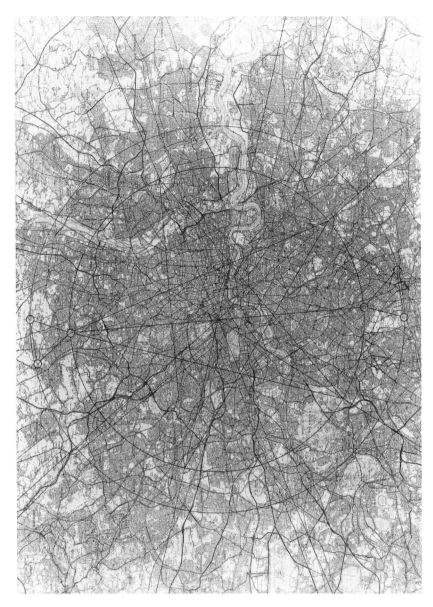

Illustration 20 (view on side):
The 5 point star. Mark points are St. Mary's East Barnet. St Gabriels Wanstead,
St. Dunstan's Bellingham Green, a mound in Sion House gounds, Horsendon Hill
Greenford. Junction points are St. George's Nine Elms, Tower Hill, Highbury
Hill, St. Andrews Frognal and Abbotsbury Rd Holland Pk.Note how the all the
main axes of the figure run almost parallel to many of London's Roman Roads.

72

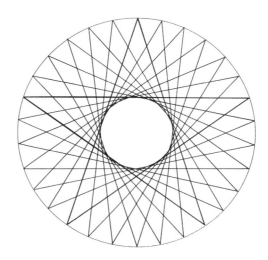

Illustration 21: One of the more complex patterns in the Earthstars geometry defined by London's sacred sites; a thirty-point star.

Illustration 22: Several of the Earthstars patterns overlaid to show the complexity of the design.

CHAPTER ELEVEN

THE HOLY GRAIL,
THE HOLY SPIRIT
AND THE DIVINE FEMININE

I realise that the mysteries of Camelot Moat have led us into rather esoteric territory. I make no apologies for that. It seems to come with the territory. Isn't it rather synchronistic though, that a place called Camelot has led us specifically to the mysteries of The Round Table and The Holy Grail.

So what is The Grail ?

In alchemy, the grail is described as the philosopher's stone, Lapis Philosophorum.

Amongst the Christian expressions of the Grail are: The Cup of the last supper or the bowl used by Joseph of Arimathea to collect the blood of Christ at his crucifixion.

In many of the Grail Romances, it is a cup that appears as one of a number of objects carried in procession through the court of the Fisher King. The other objects, known as The Grail Hallows, are a spear, a sword and a plate or dish, as well as the grail cup.

They correspond to the four suits of the tarot which, in turn, are traditionally held to relate to the four alchemical elements, Earth, Air, Fire and Water, as well as the four seasons and four cardinal directions.

They also relate to four degrees of initiation in The Secret Grail tradition.
Swords are the Initiation and path of The King, Arthur, who drew the sword from the stone.

Wands are the initiation and mysteries of Merlin.

Pentacles are the initiation and journey of the Grail Knigh.

Cups are the intiation and mysteries of The Goddess, or The Queen, Guinevere.

If the tarot Ace of Cups represents the Grail cup, even its most basic symbolism is revealing. It relates to the direction of the West, the element water, the emotions in general (love in particular), and the season of Autumn. As with all Aces, it represents a beginning, a source relative to these attributes. So the simplest tarot meaning of the Grail cup could be said to refer to 'the source of the Waters of Life.'

That ties is interestingly with The Elucidation's Grail Maidens who hold the Grail chalices and are guardians of all the waters of life at their literal sources, wells and springs.

Important though that insight is, let's move on.

Generally, the grail Romances are believed to be re-workings of much older manuscripts of pre-Christian origin and the item most frequently cited as the forerunner of the grail is the Cauldron of the Celtic Goddess Cerridwen.

Cerridwen's cauldron is an ancient feminine symbol of renewal, rebirth, transformation and inexhaustible abundance. In it, she brewed a potion that bestowed inspiration, knowledge and wisdom. Such was its potency that it was said to restore life to the corpse of any dead warrior paced in it.

It is therefore the primary female symbol of the pre-Christian world, and represents the womb of the Great Goddess from which all things are born and reborn, again and again.

In **The Elucidation**, the grail is the Maiden's Golden Cup and/or its contents, representing in the broadest sense, the 'Waters of Life.'

In both Cerridwen's cauldron and the Maiden's cup, we have examples of a vessel that contains a substance that gives life and renews it.

This gives us a variation on the Sang Real – Holy Grail/Holy Blood theme that Baigent, Leigh, Lincoln and others have interpreted as a covert reference to a secret blood line of Christ.

In the bowl of the crucifixion, the 'Waters of Life' simply become the life-blood of Christ to lend a Christian understanding to the concept.

My own personal belief is that the concept of the Grail probably originated with a pre-Christian spiritual tradition in which the 'Waters of Life' were comprehended as a synonym for the universal and planetary life force which invisibly exists all around us and is the hidden life-support system of every living thing.

As we have seen, this ties in with an understanding of The Elucidation's Grail, the symbolism of the Tarot's Grail Cup and my personal experience and understanding of the Earthstars significance.

So far, unless I am mistaken, the life-force is not something science has developed a device to detect or measure in any way that would be satisfactory to a sceptical scientific mind. But we do have a vast repository of knowledge on it within the doctrines of such subjects as Yoga where it is known as Prana, or from Taoist practices like Tai Chi, Chi Kung (Qi gong) and acupuncture where it is understood as Chi, Ki or Qi.

In the native traditions of the Pacific, it is known as Mana, commonly described as "the stuff of which magic is formed", as well as "the substance of which souls are made."

Thanks to George Lucas, it has even entered popular culture as The Force in Star Wars.

Chi has been studied for thousands of years, in China, Japan, India and Tibet. It is the energy of life itself, recognized as the balance of Yin and Yang (male and female, positive and negative), which flows through everything in creation. Chi is the foundation of many health and fitness practices such as Massage, Yoga, Martial Arts, Reiki, Feng Shui and Acupressure.

As Chi, Ki or Qi, the life force is both male and female, yin and yang. The concept of The Holy Spirit, the active force of creation and renewal, is rather different from Chi, Ki, or Prana, as it seems to be a distinctly creative aspect of the life-force, active in the world at large, and is widely regarded as specifically feminine.

In the Druid tradition, the term for life-force is Nwyvre. As this extract from an article about a French church, L'eglise de St. Gregoire-du-Vievre, states, a lot of European words derive from the nwyvre of the Celts, most of them bearing the feminine pre-fix La.

"On retrouve d'ailleurs en Europe beaucoup de mots dérivants de la Nwyvre des Celtes: la Vosvre, la Vaur, la Voivre, la Vièvre, Vabres, Vouivre, Guivre,…."

The Hindu religion has a valuable contribution to add to this subject, too, because it holds a similar concept and its beliefs are of immense antiquity. The origins of Hinduism can be traced back to the religion's roots in the Indus valley civilization, 4000 to 2200 BCE.

In Hinduism, the universe is the manifestation of the creative power (Shakti) of Brahman, whose essence is absolute existence, consciousness, and bliss. Shakti, the creative power of God is recognized by Hindus as the female principle or the motherly aspect of nature, since to Hindus, all created forms proceed from the womb of the great mother.

Shakti is therefore, both the concept of the Mother Goddess, Mother Nature and the personification of divine feminine creative power. Not only is the Shakti responsible for creation, she is also the agent of all change and evolution and the presence of the Goddess in the world.

78

Illustration 24: The Grail Hallows as the tarot Aces, including of course, the golden Grail Cup.

Shakti is a sort of Hindu Holy Spirit and the comparison goes a lot further than you might initially expect. Because the Christian Holy Spirit, although a major element in the dominant patriarchal religions of the west, is secretly feminine.

A lot of people find this extremely hard to accept. Yet the majority of the evidence comes from the scriptures.

Exhibit 'A' is the word most frequently used to represent the Holy spirit. In the Old Testament and the Dead Sea Scrolls, the Holy Spirit was known by the Hebrew/Aramaic word, Ruach or Ruach Ha Kodesh.

In many languages (but not English), nouns are allocated a gender, presumably dependant on their essential nature or perceived attributes.

The word Ruach, meaning 'spirit', 'breath of life' or 'soul' is of the feminine gender and you don't have a feminine noun for something that is masculine.

The implication is that the Holy Spirit is a female presence. In fact, it is the presence of the hidden Goddess.

Ruach was translated into Latin as Spiritus Sanctus and, in the process underwent an unfortunate, early gender re-alignment, ending up as masculine.

The Hebrew word Shekinah, which is frequently used to describe the presence of God, is also feminine.

A third example of the divine feminine principle being lost in translation is the word Elohim. It came to mean "God," male and singular, whereas in fact the word in Hebrew is feminine and plural.

Not to put too fine a point on it, Elohim correctly translated means 'Goddesses.' That's right. In the original Hebrew passages containing the word Elohim, God was actually an undefined number of

Goddesses and everyone who could read and understand Hebrew at that time would have been in no confusion over the word's meaning; goddesses !

Remember that for around 3,000 years, the Hebrews worshipped female deities which were later obliterated by extreme pressure from the male-dominated priesthood.

In **The Secret Doctrine** by Helene Petrova Blavatsky, she informs us:

"The translators of the bible have crowded out of sight and suppressed every reference to the feminine form of deity. They have, as we just seen, translated the feminine plural of Elohim by the masculine singular of GOD. But they have done more than this; They have carefully hidden the fact that the word ruach – the 'spirit' – is feminine. And that consequently the Holy Ghost of the New Testament is a feminine potency."

There is even one direct reference to The Holy Spirit being a woman. In the **Nag Hammadi scrolls**, Phillip the Apostle gives us his considered opinion on the notion that the Holy Spirit played a part in Mary's conception. He is quoted as saying:

"When did a woman ever conceive of another woman?"

Obviously, he understood that the Ruach, or Holy Spirit was specifically a feminine presence. According to J. J. Hurtak, this is the one time in the Christian scriptures where the Holy Ghost is referred to clearly and directly as a 'woman', leading Hurtak to comment;

"It is no wonder that Phillip's gospel is excluded from the patriarchal canon."

Yet, once the shock of this revelation has worn off, it begins to make sense of things that were previously unfathomable mysteries.

For instance, in the light of this information, we can now

appreciate the Holy Trinity as a slightly more normal family unit, Father, Son and Divine Mother.

Much more believable than Father, Son and something that's deeply suspicious, but we'll keep it under wraps, throw a sheet over it, call it The Holy Ghost and hope no-one asks too many questions.

Phillip, it has to be remembered, walked with the historical Jesus, so if he clearly understood that the Holy Spirit was feminine, we can assume that, from the very beginning, the original teachings of Jesus, while he was alive, understood, acknowledged and possibly included this feminine principle.

This means that the Christian tradition, as Helena Blavatsky claims, conceals a goddess disguised as the Holy Spirit, strongly associated with Mary, and who may have played an important role in the religion from its earliest days.

A clue to who this goddess may have originally been lies in the descent of the Holy Spirit as a dove.

The dove was the symbol of Asherah, the Mother Goddess of the Sumerians, Canaanites and Phoenicians, who were neighbours of the biblical Jewish race. Anyone alive at that time, in that area, would have understood a reference to the Dove as meaning The Mother Goddess, Asherah, who was known elsewhere by many names including Astarte, Ishtar, Baalat and others.

Clay tablets dating from as far back as 1400 B.C, show Asherah's name written in a language similar to biblical Hebrew. Her full name is "Lady Asherah of the Sea" since she ruled the oceans and the Earth, while her consort, El, ruled the Heavens.

Asherah is a well-documented goddess of the Semitic pantheon and archaeologists have uncovered Hebrew settlements which prove the goddesses Asherah and Astarte-Anath were routinely worshipped.

In fact, for around 3,000 years, the Hebrews worshipped several

Goddesses who the male-dominated priesthood later attempted to obliterate from memory and history.

According to the Bible itself, in the ninth century BCE, Asherah was officially worshipped in Israel. Her cult was supposedly imported by Jezabel who was Phoenician.

Other biblical references either dismissively acknowledge her worship, or because she was associated with sacred pillars, poles or staffs (of wisdom, power and healing), attempt to link her name to these objects, rather than the goddess herself.

It is only a short step from the idea of Mother Goddess to Divine Mother and so the sacred feminine concealed within Christianity has evolved through an association with Mary.

The weight of evidence is convincing.

Despite the male gender of the phrase "Spiritus Sanctus" the writings of the Catholic fathers present the vision of The Holy Spirit as "the Bride" or as the "Mother Church." Both feminine.

This is supported from more esoteric sources. William Stirling in **The Cannon** refers to;

"Bride, the third person of the Triad " (page216) and "The Great Mother Earth, or the heavenly spouse of The Logos, called The Holy Ghost" (page278).

In the Eastern Church, The Holy Spirit was always considered to have an essentially feminine nature. Clement of Alexandria states that *'she' is 'an indwelling Bride'.*

Most significant are the content of the Dead Sea Scrolls, which have demonstrated that far more early Christians than we would have imagined regarded the Holy Spirit as feminine.

The Acts of Thomas, a 3rd century scroll of mystical Coptic

83

Christianity, gives a graphic account of the Apostle Thomas' travels to India, and contains prayers invoking the Holy Spirit as:

"the Mother of all creation" and "compassionate mother,"

Other Coptic Christian writings link the: *"spirit of Spirit"* with the *"Spirit of the Divine Mother."*

In fact, there is no clearer evidence about the feminine aspect of the Holy Spirit than from the Coptic-Gnostics. Their gospels even include Jesus actually referring to The Holy Spirit as his mother, re-enforcing this perceived link with Mary:

"Even so did my mother, the Holy Spirit, take me by one of my hairs and carry me away to the great mountain Tabor."

The same theme is echoed in another Nag Hammadi discovery, The Secret Book of James, where Jesus refers to himself as: *"the son of the Holy Spirit."*

The weight of evidence for a feminine Holy Spirit who is an aspect of The Divine Mother, either as Mary or a pre-Christian Mother Goddess with similar qualities, is overwhelming.

However, the shroud of the Holy Spirit hides yet another female.

In the Gnostic traditions and in the Eastern Orthodox churches of Greece and Coptic Egypt, the Holy Spirit is openly acknowledged as Sophia, Wisdom.

Wisdom in the bible is definitely feminine, like the Holy Spirit. The Old Testament word for "wisdom" is chokmah which has a feminine ending. Translating wisdom into Greek makes the connection obvious because it then becomes Sophia, the name of the goddess herself.

In many biblical references, Wisdom is clearly stated to be female, as in the references below from Proverbs.

"Doth not wisdom cry? and understanding put forth her voice? She standeth in the top of high places, by the way in the places of the paths.

She crieth at the gates, at the entry of the city, at the coming in at the doors. Unto you, O men, I call; and my voice is to the sons of man. O ye simple, understand wisdom: and, ye fools, be ye of an understanding heart."

Further evidence that the notion of Wisdom as feminine is universal comes from the Tibetan tradition, where ancient teachings have survived into modern times with no attempts to suppress the divine feminine (at least not until the invasion by Communist China who have attempted to ruthlessly stamp out every trace of Tibetan culture and religion). In Tibetan Buddhism, wisdom is personified by the goddess, Tara.

In the scriptures, Wisdom, is the Lady that inspires men to be good, righteous, wise, and to perform virtuous deeds.

Doesn't that sound uncannily like "The Lady" whom the Knights of the Round table pledged to serve ?

Or 'The Inspirer' of the druidic tradition, The White Goddess ?

The connection is compounded by Dr Hugh J. Schonfield, one of the scholars who worked on the Dead Sea Scrolls.

In his book **The Essene Odyssey** he makes the claim that The Templars, who are actually called The Grail Knights in the later Grail Romances, covertly worshipped Sophia, the Goddess of Wisdom.

This claim originates from the Inquisition of the Knights Templar in the 1300s, when some Templars are recorded as confessing to the worship of an idol they called 'Baphomet.'

According to Dr. Schonfield, the name 'Baphomet' can be decoded using the Atbash cipher, which substitutes the first letter of the

Hebrew alphabet for the last, the second for the second last, and so on. 'Baphomet' subjected to this system can be interpreted as 'Sophia.'

A second theory on the origins of 'Baphomet' yields a similar and supporting result. Baphomet itself is a name of otherwise unestablished origin, but it could be formed from two Greek words, 'Baph' and 'Metis', which together might be interpreted as 'Baptism of Wisdom.' Does this hint at a Templar Tradition of initiation into a cult of the Goddess of Wisdom through a literal baptism? Possibly similar to de Mandeville's initiatory death in Camelot Moat's well ?

Where the Knights Templar could have acquired knowledge of this concealed cult of the Goddess is debatable, but there's every possibility that it came from their sojourns to The Holy Land.

It is precisely the same kind of covert goddess worship which is at the root of the Secret Tradition in Arthurian Legend and the Grail Romances.

Incidentally, Sir Geoffrey de Mandeville is known to have had very odd associations with the Templars, to say the least. He was said not to be a member of the order, yet on his death following the seige of Burwell Castle in 1144, a group of Templars rode from London to Mildenhall to claim his body.

On their return to the Temple, instead of giving him a burial, they hung his corpse in an apple tree where it remained for 19 years. The explanation for these weird events is supposedly the fact that he was excommunicated and could not be buried on hallowed ground. But that does nothing to shed light on why his body was hung in an apple tree for so long.

He was finally laid to rest in 1163. If you visit the Temple Church, Sir Geoffrey is now one of Knights whose stone effigies take pride of place on the floor in the centre of the round church, an extraordinary honour for someone supposedly not a Templar. In Templar traditions, being buried in the round church was considered as good as being buried in Jerusalem itself.

So what, as we approach the end of the chapter, does all this add up to ?

Well, we can draw some very interesting conclusions and make some bold claims, though I have to admit, we can't prove any of this conclusively.

What we can do is raise a series of questions, all beginning 'what if ?'

What if the Holy Spirit and the planetary and universal life-force are one in the same ?

From this evidence, it seems a distinct probability.

What if the guardians of the grail, who are always women, re-flect the feminine nature of the Holy Spirit and the Goddess archetypes it manifests as ?

What if the Grail Romances actually do conceal a secret tradi-tion which revered the Earth Mother or a pre-Christian Mother arche-type as a Goddess ?

What if one of the mysteries of Christianity is that the Holy Spirit is the feminine principle and the last remaining vestige of God-dess worship in Christianity?

What if senior members of the churches are aware of this and still revere her through the cult of Mary ?

What if Christ's reference to The Holy Spirit as his mother indi-cates that the original Christians were aware of this and that it was part of their beliefs ?

What if places with a high incidence of Marian reverence and a high number of churches dedicated to Mary (like Britain and Ireland) were places where worship of this Goddess - or at least the divine fem-inine princeiple - was dominant?

What if the ancient churches dedicated to Mary The Divine Mother stand on sites previously sacred to the Earth Mother or the Goddess?

What if the Holy Spirit, the Holy Grail, the life-force and the Goddess are all one?

Let us ask the Grail seeker's question: "Who does the Grail serve ?"

They serve all, equally, as the Grail should.

Illustration 25: The Grail maiden and one of her counterparts in the Tarot, The Queen of Cups.

CHAPTER TWELVE

THE MYSTERY OF TRENT PARK'S GREAT PYRAMIID

Having revealed the secret of The Grail, we come to the mystery of Trent Park's Great Pyramid, yet another enigma of the local landscape around Camelot Moat.

If you know Trent Park in Cockfosters, you'll be wondering what I'm talking about. There isn't a pyramid anywhere in the grounds. Well, not one you can see, anyway. Here's the explanation.

In 1934, Sir Phillip Sassoon purchased three stone monuments from a sale at Wrest Park in Bedfordshire, home of the powerful de Grey family, Earls of Kent, from 1280 to the 19th Century.

The largest was a tall obelisk which he ordered to be erected on the northern boundary of his Trent Park estate, on the edge of the woods bordering Ferny Hill Farm. It carries an inscription;

"To the memory of the birth of George Grey, Early of Harold, son of Henry and Sophia, Duke and Duchess of Kent, 1702."

The smallest was a monument dedicated to Henry Duke of Kent and dated 1740. Sir Phillip placed it at the western end of the impressive avenue of trees that line the main drive towards his Mansion. These days, it's where the drive forks left to the café car park or right to the college.

The third, a tall column topped by a stone pineapple and commemorating Jemima Crewe, Duchess of Kent, stands at the other end of the avenue, in the middle of the drive that leads to the Mansion and Middlesex University Campus.

These latter two are set exactly half a mile apart, but there are far stranger facts about the way Sir Phillip had these monuments positioned.

If you find a large-scale map of the park, then draw lines to link the three monuments, you'll find that they form a perfect right-angled triangle.

That's just the beginning. This triangle is the basis of some quite remarkable figures.

Place a compass point on the pineapple column that occupies the right angle, and set the compass to draw two circles with radii to the other two monuments. You'll be amazed to see that you end up with two concentric circles identical to the foundational 'master pattern' of the Earthstars geometry featured in Chapter 10.

This is astonishing. Sir Phillip Sassoon set up this pattern nearly fifty years before I discovered the identical pattern in London's Earthstars' geometry.

Was he a member of a secret society who worked with and understood these matters ?

Was he creating his own Earthstar, Stargate or Round Table on his estate ?

It is definitely not a chance formation, because another important design is involved as you will see if you extend the base line of the triangle across the inner circle. Where the line meets the circle, draw a line up to the obelisk to create a mirror image of the first triangle. You're now looking at a near-perfect side view/elevation of The Great Pyramid of Giza.

There is some inconsistency depending on which maps are used. The OS 1:25,000 scale gives a 52/53 degree angle for the slope of the pyramid's sides. The Geographer's A-Z, 9-sheet map of North London makes it nearer 51/52 degrees.

Either one is close enough. The actual angle of the real pyramid is usually quoted as 51degrees 51minutes so it is slightly nearer 52 than 51degrees. Close enough for us to recognise the distinctive Great Pyramid profile anyway.

As well as having accurate dimensions, the way the pyramid fits in with other features of the local landscape is rather interesting, too. It looks like the design dictates the orientation and position of several other geographical features.

The pyramid's base sits on the main entrance drive that leads along the avenue of trees from the Car Park to the University complex. Extended in either direction, this base line connects to places that have already cropped up earlier in the book. To the west, the line goes to Whitings Hill, off Mays Lane in Barnet, a significant mark point on one of the Camlet Moat leys. To the East, it goes to Forty Hall, near where Mr. Mahoney found King Arthur's Cross.

The vertical axis up to the obelisk demonstrates more precise correlations.

Extended south, it coincides with most of Snakes Lane (including the original section diverted for the Piccadilly Line), then runs directly alongside Chase Road right up to the site of the South Gate of Enfield Chase not far from Southgate tube station.

It looks like this could have been an ancient track through Enfield Chase from the South Gate and must have once crossed the entire Royal hunting ground, because to the north of the obelisk, the alignment picks up the course of another path which runs from a lay-by in Ferny Hill down a footpath past Ash Wood.

The western side of the pyramid, runs almost directly along the course of a path that exits the woods near the park café and becomes the road down to the main gate. This alignment can be extended to Christ Church in Chalk Lane Cockfosters.

The eastern slope of the pyramid extends directly to the bronze-age hill fort, whose remains can be still be seen near the clubhouse of Bush Hill Park Golf Club.

There's one final important path upon which the obelisk sits. It is not connected to the pyramid profile, but runs alongside the boundary between the woods and a field belonging to Ferny Hill Farm.

The important thing about this path is that it aligns, through the obelisk, to a midsummer sunrise position. At dawn on midsummer's day, the shadow of the obelisk points directly down this path.

Some of these tracks may have existed since the earliest foundation of The Chase, so it raises the question of whether Sir Phillip Sassoon actually created this design when he sited his three monuments, or whether he was building upon something that already existed here from an indeterminable date.

Despite the fact that the geometry is identical, I don't think Sir Phillip can have been aware of the Earthstars network concealed within the London landscape. It is too vast and complex.

The simplest explanation is that his intention was to replicate the great pyramid geometry which is based, like Stonehenge, upon the same foundational pattern as the London Earth-stars. This could be the result of his interest in all things Egyptian developed eleven years earlier when he was present at the opening of Tutankhamen's tomb. Or is that is too simple for such a significant design?

The alternative is that Sassoon's pyramid pattern demonstrates an awareness of the art of sacred geometry, an understanding of geomancy and an appreciation of the significance of the relationship of the two concentric circles, which is unique and widely considered to be the essence of the most important construction of sacred geometry.

It is based on the Squared Circle, which symbolically reconciles the two opposites of the square and the circle, by creating them with equal circumference or area.

A square on the inner circle represents the Earth, with its four directions, four seasons, and readily calculable dimensions.

The outer circle represents either the heavens or the infinite spiritual realms, as its symbolism is eternal, with no beginning, no end. All its calculations are considered to be ultimately incalculable since they rely upon the infinitely extendable irrational number, Pi, which it self is ultimately incalculable.

It is understandably that a piece of geometry said to represent a union of Heaven and Earth should be used as the basis for a temple ground plan.

This connection between Heaven and Earth is demonstrated re-markably well in the design of the Great Pyramid.

The pyramid's base stands on the square of the Earth while its point, touches the circle of the heavens.

So what's this design doing in Trent Park ?

Well, here the circles encompass almost the whole park, so Sir Phillip Sassoon may have been utilising the design to cast a general protective and beneficial influence over his estate.

It is a well-known and surprising fact that the geometry of the Great Pyramid produces remarkable effects: A cardboard pyramid, for instance, can sharpen blunt razor blades placed within it.

Whether it produces similar unusual energies when utilised as a landscape design is another matter, but that is the theory behind this kind of scheme.

You can call it a Landscape Temple, a Round Table, a Stargate or "magic circle," it implies knowledge of how to plug into the univer-sal and planetary life-force – a sort of Science of the Holy Spirit, in Christian terms.

That in turn suggests Sir Phillip might have been a member of some society in possession of this esoteric knowledge, perhaps Masonic, perhaps Rosicrucian, perhaps some other stream of the Western Mystery Traditions.

He is no longer around to tell us, so we'll never find out for sure.

An alternative suggestion is that the deliberate, precise and meaningful positioning of these monuments may have been designed by Sassoon as a clue to the location of something else.

What, for instance, is in the eastern woods of Trent Park at the eastern base corner of the pyramid, a remote spot not marked by a monument?

I have traced the location (close to the horse-riding track) and found evidence of brickwork at ground level. Something is there beneath the ground. What is it ? Did another monument once stand there or is something now buried there?

What does the obelisk point to on midsummer's day when the dawn light casts its shadow down the sunrise path?

Is there anything significant in the woods to correspond with the location of the pyramid's King's Chamber ?

Could it be that Sassoon found De Mandeville's treasure (or something else) in the well, and not being in need of more wealth himself, concealed it again in his grounds, for someone else to find. Then left a clue to its whereabouts in the form of the pyramid and squared circle hidden within the estate's layout?

Highly unlikely, I admit, but you never know.

If you're a fan of Graham Phillip's books as I am (in particular The Search for the Grail + The Templars and the Ark of the Covenant), you'll know that this kind of thing does happen.

Or is there another explanation for this enigmatic geometry that no-one has yet considered ?

Illustration 26: The obelisk, which marks the uppermost point of Sir Phillip Sassoon's mysterious pyramid.

Illustration 27: The Pineapple column which marks the centre of the pyramid's base line.

Illustration 28:
The triangle formed by the three monuments that Sir Phillip Sassoon bought from Wrest Park in 1934.
All three sides of the triangle follow the course of various paths, tracks or roads into or through Trent Park as if it is an intrinsic part of the local landscape, not a super-imposed addition.
The base line folows the avenue of trees along the main drive.
The vertical line to the obelisk follows the course of Snakes Lane a the path past Ash Wood to the north. It is also aligned to the many paths running parrallel to Snakes Lane.
The hypoteneuse follows the path through oak wood to the cafe where it becomes the road from the car park to the main gate.

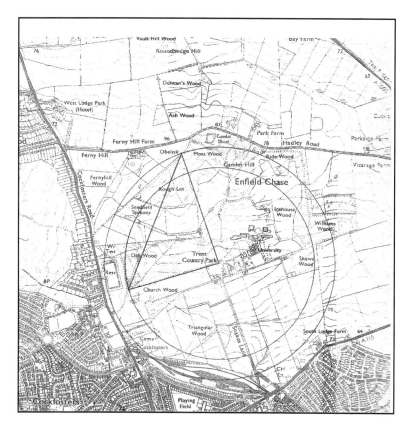

Illustration 29:
**Circles centred on the pineapple column, with radii to the other two monuments
produce two concentric circles with a proportional ratio identical to the foundational pattern of the London Earthstars' geometry.**

98

Illustration 30:
The mystery revealed. The three monuments were carefully positioned to create an exact replica of the profile of the Great Pyramid concealed within the landscape of Trent Park. What was Sir Phillip Sassoon's motives for doing this ?

99

CHAPTER THIRTEEN

THE SWORD IN THE STONE

Now we have a Round Table at Camelot, as well as the Earth-stars' Round Table that covers most of London.

As we've seen from Charles Williams' map, some occultists believe London itself is Camelot. So are there any other Arthurian connections to London which we should examine ?

I think there is one of great importance: the notion that King Arthur drew the sword from a stone in the churchyard of St. Paul's Cathedral.

In **La Morte D'Arthur,** Sir Thomas Mallory states very clearly that Arthur fulfilled his destiny to become King by pulling the sword from the stone;

" in the greatest church of London, whether it were Paul's or not the French book maketh no mention."

The 'French book' is a reference to a manuscript in the French Language from which Mallory purports to have transcribed elements of the story.

The greatest church in London has to be St. Paul's. Westminster Abbey was just that, an Abbey, not a church.

St. Paul's, at the time when **La Morte D'Arthur** was published, was actually the largest Protestant Cathedral church in London and probably the largest church in the entire country.

The big question is, did it ever have a megalithic stone in its churchyard that could have literally been the stone of kingship?

The surprising answer is, yes, it did. It is no longer there, of course, but strong evidence for its existence survives in the form of St. Paul's Cross.

The present St. Paul's Cross is an impressive monument to the northern side of the Cathedral, consisting of an elaborately carved fountain base, supporting a tall column topped by a gilded statue of St. Paul.

This monument is actually a memorial to a Mr H. Richards and a reminder of the original cross, as the plaque on its east side states:

"On this plot of ground stood of old, St. Paul's Cross, where amid such scenes of good and evil as make up the human affairs, the conscience of church and nation through five centuries found public utterance.
The first record of it is in 1191 and it was re-built by Bishop Kemp in 1449 and was finally removed by order of the long parliament in 1643.
This cross was perfected in its present form under the will of H. Richards, to recall and renew the ancient memories."

The reference to *"the conscience of church and nation finding public utterance"* stems from the fact that, this spot had served, for at least the previous five hundred years as a place of free speech, often used by preachers and rabble-rousers alike.

Its origins may have been considerably older. Like Parliament Hill, this was an ancient druidic place of free speech of great national importance, where meeting were held in the open, as was the druid tradition.

On this spot people would gather to discuss and resolve all manner of business, including the election of successive kings of England.

Since a stone marked the place of free speech on Parliament Hill, it would not be presumptuous to expect that one had previously stood here too and that both places had common origins as ancient druidic and truly democratic, open-air, people's parliaments.

Illustration 31: St. Paul's Cross in the churchyard to the north of the Cathedral.

Illustration 32: The original site of the cross which was known as Old Pol's Cross or Old Pol's Stump.

Luckily, the memory of the old stone has not been totally obliterated and forgotten.

It is preserved in the memory of Old Pol's Stump which is said to have originally marked this spot.

Pol's stump was said to be a stone of great antiquity, into which a Christian cross had been set.

It was common practice for ancient stones (which were presumed to be pagan relics) to be Christianised by, either being carved into a cross, or used as the base for one.

The current monument is relatively recent and does not stand on the original site of Pol's Stump, though the location of the old stone and cross is easily found.

On the 1873 Ordnance Survey map, a large octagonal area (presumably the area of the cross' base) is shown adjacent to the north east side of the cathedral. On the ground in modern times, the same octagonal plan is outlined as a pattern in the paving stones in the same location.

So having established that there was a stone in the churchyard, what else do we know about it ? Was it, for instance, associated in any way with the notion of Kingship ?

The surprising answer is yes, it was.

As I mentioned earlier, this was an ancient place of free speech, of great national importance.

On this spot was held a regular folk 'moot' where people would gather to discuss and resolve all kinds of important matters.

It is a little-known fact that, when a Coronation was in the offing, this included a vote on who might or might not become King of England.

For many years, this democratic and public election was a vitally important part of the monarch's inauguration process and absolutely necessary before any king could be crowned at Westminster.

Edward IV, Stephen, Edward The Confessor, Edmund Ironsides and many others are on record as having submitted to this public election prior to their official ceremony at Westminster.

In some respects, this suggest that St. Paul's was the more important element in the process, since there would be no ceremony at Westminster Abbey if those at St. Paul's did not approve

.

OK. So there was a stone and, amazingly, it was connected to the role of selecting the King of the Realm. It was a King Stone.

As if that is not remarkable enough, its associations with Kingship go much further and deeper.

It forms part of a ley alignment which links three of the most ancient and important sacred sites in and around London, all of them places strongly associated with the Coronation of British Monarchs.

The first is the original site of The King Stone at Kingston on Thames (from which the town takes its name). Upon this stone, no less than seven Saxon Kings were crowned.

The second is Westminster Abbey, where royalty is crowned seated upon The Stone of Scone which is set beneath The Coronation Throne (or it was until the government gave it back to Scotland in 1996).

The third, is St. Paul's, where the open-air Moot in the churchyard publicly deliberated on the pre-coronation electoral process.

At two of the three three sites, it has to be noted, ancient stones are unquestionably known to have played a major part in the ritual.

It should not be stretching the imagination to guess that the third site, St. Paul's also actually had an important ancient megalith of which Old Pol's Stump was probably a remnant

The alignment of these sites was first documented as The Coronation Line in my book, **Earthstars and The Visionary Landscape.**

It isn't just defined by the three major sites already mentioned. There's a lengthy list of other mark points on the alignment, some old, some not-so-old. They include what could be a burial mound or tumulus disguised as a traffic island in Shoreditch, at Arnold Circus.

Major mark points and landmarks;

Waynflete's Tower and Moat, Esher (private property).
All Saints' Church, the original site of The Kingstone at Kingston-upon-Thames.
One of the highests points in Richmond Park.
Putney Heath.
The Peace Pagoda, Battersea Park.
St. Stephen's Church in Rochester Row, SWI.
Westminster Abbey.
Houses of Parliament (palace of Westminster).
County Hall (ex- GLC HQ).
The Oxo Tower
St. Andrews-by-the-wardrobe and St. Ann's Blackfriars.
St. Paul's Cathedral.
St. Vedast, Foster Lane EC2.
St. Mary Aldermanbury (ruins, now a pleasant garden, at the corner of Love Lane and Aldermanbury, near The Guild Hall.
Moorgate station, the former site of a nunnery.
The Chapel of the Open Book, Wilson Street EC2.
Wilson Street Chapel next to the Flying Horse, (also on the line).

The Mount, Arnold Circus (also on Watkins' Strand
Ley).
St. Matthew's Church at Bethnal Green.
The possible site of The Leyton Stone (a fourth stone on the
alignment !)
Hilltop and crossroads marked by the Maypole Pub at
Chigwell Row, Essex;
Extends SW to Durleston Head Dorset.

The other important feature of this alignment is that it is generally orientated in the direction of the midsummer sunrise.

Local topography at individual locations along its length may
mean the sighting line may vary a little, from place to place, but overall
the general orientation is to 51 degrees E of N. The midsummer sunrise
angle.

This is further circumstantial evidence for the existence of the
stone. There is a well-documented precedent of megalithic 'King
Stones' being set a short distance outside a stone circle to mark the
midsummer sunrise alignment, as at The Rollright Stones in Warwick-
shire and the Hele Stone at Stonehenge.

This midsummer alignment raises the question of whether the
Kings' Stone at Kingston on Thames and, more importantly, the Kings'
Stone of Pol's Stump at St. Paul's, fulfilled the same role and are in-
dicative of the site of a stone circle nearby.

Certainly E.O. Gordon in her book Prehistoric London, main-
tained that there had been stone circles atop Ludgate hill where St.
Paul's now stands, as well as at Westminster. If there were, they are
long gone, probably broken up to build houses and city walls.

Occasionally, such monuments are remembered in place names
and here's a possible example from quite near to St. Paul's.

A little to the north of Ludgate Hill is the site of St Mary's
Staininghage at St Alban's place. The actual church no longer exists
having been destroyed in the Great Fire.

Today it is just a small grassy oasis in the city, most often used by sandwich-munching office workers on their lunch break.

The information board here tells us the name Staininghage is Saxon and may relate to people *"who came from Staines."*

This suggested derivation of the name struck me as being rather too naive to be correct. It just didn't sound right. Besides, I knew the name Staines itself derives, broadly speaking, from the Saxon word for stones and specifically from The Negen Stanes, (the nine stones), a megalithic circle that local researchers locate at the site of the road island on the A30 to the west of Staines Bridge.

So if Staines itself is named after a local stone circle, it is equally feasible that this similarly named church on top of Ludgate Hill could be, too.

Its name could equally mean 'the church of the people of the stones,' suggesting that there were still some remnants of a megalithic monument on Ludgate Hill in the Saxon period. Possibly, they were the stones of the circle of which Pol's Stump was the King Stone.

The evidence is growing. Now we have an actual stone, in a location related to the process of selecting a king, in a known alignment of other proven Coronation sites, on a midsummer sunrise alignment and close by, is a church whose name derives from a Saxon phrase meaning people of the stones.

To understand how all these elements fit together, we first have to take a look at the connections between the King and the Sun, because the two seem interestingly and inextricably linked in many traditions.

In fact, in many cultures, the king is an embodiment of the sun god. The Pharaohs, as well as the Inca rulers of South America, were "Suns of The Son," and took the name of their Sun God as part of their official title.

Rameses is an obvious example, incorporating Ra, one of the aspects of the sun god in Egypt, in his own name. Neb Maat Ra, a.k.a. Amonhotep III, is another typical example.

In more recent times, Europe, too, has its Sun King in the flamboyant Louis XIV.

Moreover, the crown which represents Kingship in many places is clearly a symbol of the Sun. Gold is the metal traditionally associated with the Sun and the crown's most recognisable feature are its radiating spikes clearly designed to represent the Sun's rays. So the King wears a solar crown.

The reason for this close relationship shared by the Sun and the king can be easily explained.

In a very real way, the Sun is the true ruler of the land. It is the Sun's relationship with the Earth that rules (or regulates) life on Earth, governing the length of our days and nights, the length of the year, the cycles of the four seasons and the growth of crops and plant life in all lands.

This would have been an obvious fact to our forebears whose greatest monument, Stonehenge, stands testimony to their diligent observation of the solar and lunar cycles .

Our earliest societies, therefore, must have understood this relationship between the Sun, as the real power in the land, and the King, who wields power on a temporary basis, acting as an earthly representative of the Sun and perhaps being considered even the Sun God incarnate.

In the light of these Sun King associations, we can guess at the symbolism to be gleaned from a combination of a midsummer sunrise line and an alignment of coronation sites.

Both can be interpreted as marking a rise to power.

Illustration 33:
The King Stone at Kingston-upon-Thames. A coronation Stone upon which seven
Saxon Kings were crowned. It no longer stands on its original location which is
believed to have been in the area of the nearby Parish Church. In fact, for some
time, I believe it was kept in the church.

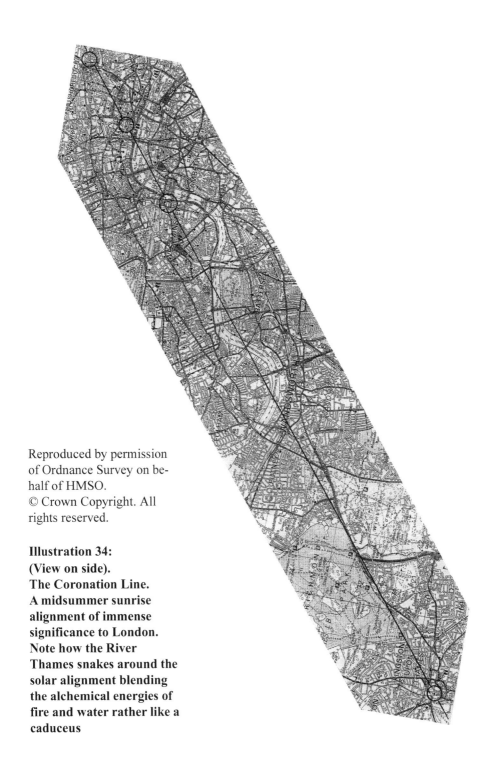

Illustration 34:
(View on side).
The Coronation Line.
A midsummer sunrise
alignment of immense
significance to London.
Note how the River
Thames snakes around the
solar alignment blending
the alchemical energies of
fire and water rather like a
caduceus

At the midsummer solstice, the sun rises at its highest point in the Eastern sky, reaches its zenith (highest point) in the midday sky and is about to begin its reign over summer, the season where it is at the height of its power.

So the midsummer solstice would be a very auspicious time for any King to be crowned and come to power.

But what do straight lines upon the landscape have to do with it and why do rulers of all types share a common etymological root which gives us such words as regal, Rex, Regina, regulations, La regle (French for ruler), Rig (Celtic for King), regime, royal and Reich, to name but a few ?

A clue lies in the ancient Chinese art of Feng Shui, a form of geomancy that can trace its origins back over 3,000 years and deals with the unseen life-force within the landscape.

The only straight alignments found in Feng Shui, radiate out from the Emperor's palace, like rays around the sun. They are exclusively associated with the ruler of the domain and represent the King's rule, and a mystical means of maintaining order in his society.

At the Temple of The Sun at Cusco in Peru, the association is even clearer. It has 40 alignments radiating out from the temple to surrounding shrines and other sacred sites, all of which obviously represent radiating lines of light and power from the sun temple.

Presumably, any Emperor, King or High Priest employing the same symbolism was attempting to somehow align himself with the power of the true ruler of the land, the sun.

If you think this may not be a reasonable conclusion to jump to, old Louis XIV provides us with another piece of evidence that it is. He ordered a series of alignments to be created, radiating out from his palace at Versailles and, since he was widely known as The Sun King, there are no prizes for guessing what they might represent.

Indeed, many of the great houses and palaces of Europe have similar linear alignments landscaped into the local terrain. Human rulers make straight lines just as wooden, plastic and metal ones do.

As we have seen, the general principle behind them appears to be an attempt to align the ruler, whether High Priest, King or Emperor, with the true ruler of the land, the sun.

Does this practice, somehow harness a real power connected to the life-force of the land?

If it does, the Sun King's Coronation line through St. Paul's, Westminster Abbey and The King Stone may incorporate some mystical or spiritual aspect of solar power.

In this respect, it is worth noting that the name Pol's Stump may not be a corruption of Paul, as most people believe.

The name is more generally known as "Old Pol" and when I first heard it, I felt it was more likely to have derived from Apollo, the sun god in the Greek Pantheon (It is known the British druids were conversant in ancient Greek).

Another researcher in this field, Steve Ash, added to this insight with the information that the name Pol is the Old Germanic nickname for Polder or Balder, an Apollo-like Nordic Sun god and a favourite of the Pagan East Saxons who were the first to re-occupy London after the Romans left. That could account for his association here. Either derivation fits rather well with the general sun king/ sun god/solar ley theme of this chapter.

However, what none of this explains is what drawing the sword from the stone actually signifies.

As a long term student of the Tarot, I started to think in terms of tarot symbolism. It turned out to be quite revealing and surprisingly relevant to the subjects that have arisen here.

Obviously, swords are a Tarot suit and a single sword is the Ace; the beginning of a successful enterprise through a determined act of will.

A single stone could be the Ace of Pentacles, part of the suit representing the element of Earth. The Ace could be thought of as a new auspicious material beginning.

I decided that pulling the sword from the stone could be translated as drawing on a power in the Earth through an act of will. The power that is drawn in this instance is the solar king energy of the alignment. That raises the possibility that the sword is actually a symbol for the power of the alignment, the King's Coronation Ley.

The sword of Kingship is the power in the ley.

Whoever draws that power into himself, through an act of will, can use it to rule the domain.

Dowsers do confirm that these energy lines respond to thought and can be stopped, diverted, amplified or whatever by thought or will. Is that the secret of the sword in the stone ?

Is the sword the power in this solar axis of sovereignty?

Can that power be drawn out through the stone of kingship? I don't see why not.

The other two Coronation Stones on the alignment, Westminster's Stone of Scone and the Kingston King Stone, both were believed to bestow the power of kingship upon the rightful monarch.

Why shouldn't this one ?

Illustration 35:
Old maps of the area show 'The Mount' as an ancient mound. Is it still here at
Arnold Circus incorporated into this traffic island. It is near a junction of three
Roman Roads and is a focus for several ley alignments, including the Coronation
Line and a line that includes the former sites of two other mounds, one at Pen-
tonville, the other at Primose Hill. Is it an ancient burial mound of a local King or
Queen ? Records tell us it has been "levelled." I imagine it may have once been
considerably bigger, probably on a scale with Merlin's Mound at Marlborough
School.

CHAPTER FOURTEEN

DOES ARTHUR'S STONE
STILL EXIST ?

In St. Paul's churchyard, where the legendary King Arthur pulled the sword from the stone, there really was an ancient stone.

It was subsequently replaced by "Old Pol's Cross" and it was a key point in a line of other King Stones aligned to the midsummer Solstice sunrise.

Probably this was the King Stone of a megalithic circle on Ludgate Hill. It must have been recognised as an extremely important stone, so surely it must have been preserved. Where is it now ? Does it still exist ?

Actually, within walking distance of St. Paul's there is an old stone, or at least a fragment of one, that hardly anyone notices. It is hidden away, built into a wall.

It is a stone reputed to be of considerable antiquity that fulfils all the criteria for Arthur's stone. It has known associations with the destiny of kings, a tradition that involves an interaction of a sword and stone as a qualification to leadership, and with the foundation and fate of London.

In various early records, the stone is repeatedly referred to as the Brutus Stone. These days it is more often known as The London Stone.

It is said to be the foundation stone of the city or of a temple to Diana, built here by Brutus the Trojan, grandson of Aeneas, following a vision in which the goddess instructed him to come to these islands and lay the foundations of a great empire. At least that is how the story goes, recounted by Geoffrey of Monmouth in **The History of The Kings of Britain**.

"Brutus, beyond the setting of the sun, past the realms of Gaul, there lies an island in the sea, once occupied by giants. Now it is empty and ready for your folk. Down the years this will prove an abode suited to you and your people: and for your descendants it will be a second Troy. A race of kings will be born there from your stock and the round circle of the whole earth will be subject to them."

After a lengthy and eventful journey, Brutus and his men landed at Totnes in South Devon. There a Brutus Stone, said to commemorate his landing, can still be found today on the north side of the High Street, 2 feet of it set flush into the pavement and another 20 feet reputedly buried beneath the floor of the adjacent shop.

"Brutus then called the island Britain, from his own name and his companions he called Britons. His intention was that his memory should be perpetuated by the derivation of his name."

" Once he had divided up his kingdom, Brutus decided to build a capital. In pursuit of this plan, he visited every part of the land in search of a suitable spot. He came at length to the river Thames, walked up and down its banks and so chose a spot for his purpose."

Historians, if they are aware of this foundation legend at all, dismiss it as fiction rather than fact.

As Tolkien suggested, history at its most ancient first evolves from fact into legend, then into myth.

However, in their thought-provoking book, **The Holy Kingdom**, Adrian Gilbert, Baram Blackett and Alan Wilson, the authors, maintain;

" It can be stated with confidence that in antiquity the story of the Trojan migration to Britain was accepted as fact."

If this is indeed the case, then London's foundation as a city is actually far older than is generally acknowledged and its heritage as Britain's capital dates right back to this distant era, estimated to be around 1200 BC by Lewis Thorpe in his 1966 edition of Geoffrey's work.

According to the **Agas Map of London**, dated 1633, slightly more precise dating is recorded. A panel on the map states that Brutus founded London originally as "New Troy" 1,130 years before Christ.

"This ancient and famous city of London was first founded by Brute the Trojan, in the year of the World, two thousand, eight hundred, thirty and two, and before the nativity of our Saviour Christ, one thousand one hundred and thirty. So that since the first building, it is two thousand seven hundred and sixty and three years. And afterwards repaired and enlarged by King Lud."

"New Troy my name when first my fame begun
By Trojan Brutes, when he me placed here on fruitful soyle
where the pleasant Thames doth flow."

E.O. Gordon in **Prehistoric London** (first published 1914), tells us that this tradition was never questioned until the last century, when German scholars pronounced it **"mythological myth"** and **"fabulous"** though why German scholars might concern themselves with the subject and be held as definitive authorities is something of a mystery in itself, unless it was something to do with the influence of our royal family, the Hanoverian Dynasty, who could trace their heritage from many German ancestors, but not from Brutus and his line of British Kings.

The fact that most Londoners have never heard of the London Stone, the foundation stone of their city, let alone seen it, is a natural result of this suppression of the city's foundation legend.

The evidence, not for the first time, seems to have been buried. In this case, literally.

The London Stone, possibly London's most important pre-historic relic, has been buried for the past forty years in the wall of an office block, at 111 Cannon Street, where it has remained, scarcely noticed and largely ignored.

For most of that time, the premises housed The Overseas Banking Corporation of China, but when that closed in 2006, the ground floor was taken over temporarily by a cut-price sports goods retailer. During the conversion, the shop manager had to prevent builders from trying to remove the stone and dump it in a skipful of rubble. That's how much our ancient heritage is valued these days.

Until The Museum of London were alerted to this act of wanton vandalism, they appeared to be as ignorant of the City's oldest megalith as most of the office workers who stroll past it everyday.

An inscription on a small brass plate above the stone does little to inform or educate. It gives scant information by way of an explanation for this curiosity and does not even mention its legendary status as the possible Foundation Stone of the City.

This careless irreverence follows the style of the mis- information boards at Camelot Moat, and seems to deliberately conceal far more than it informs.

" This is a fragment of the original piece of limestone once securely fixed in the ground now fronting Cannon Street Station. Removed in 1742 to the north side of the street, in 1798 it was built into the south wall of the Church of St. Swithin London Stone which stood here until demolished in 1962. Its origin and purpose is unknown but in 1188 there was a reference to Henry, son of Edwyn de Londenstane, subsequently Lord Mayor of London."

The writer of this seems, either totally unaware of the significance of the stone, or to have deliberately ignored it. With this kind of treatment, it is hardly surprising that so few people realise that London has a foundation stone at all, let alone one of such antiquity.

By contrast, in days gone by, it was held in some awe. For hundreds of years it was recognised as the symbolic authority and heart of the City of London. A stone upon which deals were forged, oaths were sworn and the point from which official proclamations were made.

This was a king's stone, fundamentally linked to the sovereignty of the land: A stone with deep spiritual significance, having been dedicated to the goddess Diana: An omphalos – the foundation stone and centre of power of the temple or city, or both – and as such, said to be imbued with the power and spirit of the entire capital.

Throughout the centuries, it was credited with mystical power over the safety, well-being and preservation of the city. An old saying tells us;

" so long as the Stone of Brutus is safe, so long shall London flourish."

Perhaps that explains why it has survived so long in an area where building stone must have been at a premium.

Even the Romans seem to have been wary of the London Stone's legendary status. When they constructed London's walls (or possibly re-fortified King Lud's), the shortage of good building stone in the area resulted in altar stones from their own temples, and occasionally statues, being unceremoniously built into the walls. Yet the London Stone was left unscathed.

For this humble chunk of sandstone to have survived the fate of every of piece of available masonry for miles around, it must have been considered of exceptional significance.

Some traditions suggest it may have been regarded as a stone of destiny and sovereignty, like the King Stone at Kingston-upon-Thames, upon which seven Saxon Kings sat to be crowned, or like the Stone of

Scone which served a similar purpose for generations of later British monarchs, fitted beneath the seat of the Coronation Throne in Westminster Abbey.

Without doubt, it was widely believed to possess the ability to bestow power. By simply striking the London Stone with a sword, a man could declare himself Lord Mayor of the City.

This was demonstrated last in 1450 when Jack Cade (or Mortimer), a Kentish insurgent, dissatisfied with the rule of Henry VI, resorted to this ancient tradition to declare himself the new ruler, then promptly began an uprising, which some believe was a pre-cursor to the War of the Roses five years later.

Of course, his actions at the London Stone has interesting parallels with the Arthurian sword-in-the-stone legend, in which Arthur draws a sword of power from a stone to prove he is the rightful king.

An observation worth mentioning here is that a belief in the London Stone's power is still evident. Great care seems to have been taken to prevent anyone else from following Jack Cade's example since the 15th century.

When it was moved from its original location in the middle of Candlewick Street (now Cannon Street) in 1798, it was placed behind steel bars set in a stone surround, where no one could lay a finger on it.

In its present resting place, it has been built into a wall, behind thick glass panels and is impossible to touch without the aid of a sledgehammer or pick-axe.

Who decided to deliberately obscure awareness of its history and power whilst at the same time demonstrating their own acknowledgement and wariness of it ?

The suggestion that the London Stone may have been an omphalos stone, the central foundation stone of the temple or city, may result from William Camden (a 16th century historian) claiming it was a particular type of Roman milestone, a milliarium, the central point from which the Roman roads radiated from the capital.

This is frequently believed in preference to any other theories merely because Camden is regarded as a credible source.

In fact, there is litle or no evidence to support his assertion and, more important, no mention of the London Stone at all from the Roman period.

My personal feelings are that The London Stone is definitely not a mere milestone or boundary stone. This is a stone of legendary power and significance.

But the idea that it is the foundation stone of Brutus' city and as well as his temple of Diana raises several questions.

Firstly, the temple of Diana was supposed to have been located in the area now occupied by St. Paul's and Brutus' city was centred around the temple.

So if the London Stone was Brutus' foundation Stone, of either the temple or the city, it should have been near St. Paul's, not at the bottom of the hill in what is now Cannon Street.

The conclusion we can draw is that, if the foundation stone legend is correct, then the stone has been moved from its original location at the top of Ludgate Hill near St. Paul's.

Of course, then we have to consider that there actually was a stone near St. Paul's, Old Pol's Stump which has the legend of being a king's stone.

Could it be that Old Pol's Stump and the Brutus/London Stone were the same stone?

The appearance of the stone itself could support this argument. Because The London Stone looks like it might be the top that has been cut off a larger stone.

Illustration 36:
The London Stone, reputedly the foundation stone of the city and possibly Arthur's Stone.

Illustration 37: The London Stone when set into the wall of St. Swithins Church, demolished in the seventies.

Illustration 38: The London Stone's location for the last forty years at 111 Cannon Street. It really deserves better and I personally think it should be moved to the site of Old Pol's Cross in St. Paul's church yard.

This has prompted some researchers to speculate that the rest of the stone still remains buried beneath the road in Cannon Street.

However, it is equally possible that the stump from which the top of the stone was severed, may have remained in St. Paul's churchyard where it subsequently became known as Old Pol's Stump, later to be Christianised as Paul's Cross.

I believe there is a distinct possibility that the Roman augers recognised the inherent power of Brutus' foundation stone and decided to claim and utilise it for themselves.

It was, after all, the city's symbol of power. By moving it from St. Paul's on Ludgate Hill and setting it up as a milliarium or their own omphalos within the walls of the Roman City of Londinium, they ritually took over the power of the city.

It may only be a theory, but if it is correct, it means The London Stone was originally in St. Paul's churchyard.

So if King Arthur really did draw his sword of power from a stone, that stone still exists.

It is the London Stone.

CHAPTER FIFTEEN

HEALING THE WASTELAND

This voyage of discovery began at Camelot Moat, a place with no obvious Arthurian associations, apart from its name. Yet is has led us to a series of astonishing new insights into the Arthurian Legends and the Mysteries of The Holy Grail.

We have found no chest of gold and precious stones in the well. Instead, we have unearthed some gems in terms of the facts about its known history and possible origins.

The accumulated facts relating to Camelot's past are intriguing to say the least. By their very nature they add fuel to the already smouldering embers of wild speculation. This is certainly a place that fires the imagination in more ways than one.

We have learnt that the earliest verifiable mention of the name Camelot here dates back to at least a generation before Mallory published his Morte D'Arthur, and local folklore tells us the name was in use 300 years earlier, prior even to Chretien De Troyes works.

But the name may be considerably older. At least one expert in these matters is on record as having said that the name Camelot at this location is **"indisputably Celtic in origin."**

That means the origins of the place may be over 2,000 years old, at the very least. So it existed well before the time of Arthur.

Add to this the opinion that it held a strategic position in the outer defenses of London, from Roman times or before, and we're looking at a location that would have been well known to any warrior king, as Arthur was.

It was also a place with many royal connections. Its pre-Con

126

quest ones are predictably hazy, but it was later given by King Stephen to Geoffrey de Mandeville, was inherited by the De Bohuns (into whose family Henry the IV married) and then, again under royal ownership, became the very centre of the royal hunting ground known as Enfield Chase.

Then there are the impressive archaeological finds, that indicate a substantial, castle-like construction on this site.

Flint stone walls "over five and a half feet thick" containing "huge stones." A massive drawbridge 38ft in length supported on oak beams a foot square. A subterranean dungeon complete with a chain still firmly affixed to the wall. A moat.

It definitely sounds like a castle, doesn't it? Though the idea of huge stones might trigger justifiable speculation that they came from a megalithic monument.

Which brings us to the idea of Camelot as a sacred site and, with or without the chest of goodies at the bottom of the well, we've discovered a wealth of spiritual treasure here.

The very atmosphere of the place seems to convince visitors it is a sacred spot, even without considering the opinions of those who feel it is a place of healing, a place of inspiration.

Those who have seen the apparitions of "Our Lady of Camelot Moat" (or the White Goddess), need no convincing of this. They have had personal proof.

Camelot's connections to the grail legends have been remarkable. A wealth of evidence exists for a secret tradition concealed within Arthurian legend, where the knights' service to The Lady hides a goddess cult in which Guinevere represents the sovereign spirit, soul and Life-Force of the land, or the White Goddess, as Robert Graves would have called her.

We've discovered that even this Camelot has a Round Table, in the form of the Earthstars' geometric web of life, upon the landscape, woven by the ancient weaver Goddesses. It is symbolic of the hidden unity which connects all things in life and harmony.

As well as finding Camelot in London, we've also discovered that when Arthur pulled his sword of power from the stone, that stone was in London. And still is.

Its original location was at St. Paul's and the Royal Line from whence he drew his power and authority is a very significant midsummer sunrise alignment through the capital; **The Earthstars' Coronation Line.**

The solar midsummer energy of this Ley could represent the sword as the power, justice and authority of the rightful ruler, which is pulled from the stone (the Earth).

It is a power connected to the megalithic science of our ancestors.

Most importantly, the secret of the Holy Grail has been de-mystified so that we can now understand that the goddess, the universal life force and the Holy Spirit are all one; three ways of relating to the elusive natural life force, each originating from different times, cultures and religions.

All are aspects of the Grail which serves all.

We can now appreciate that the wasteland is the atheist or materialist paradigm of a soul-less land, where human greed overthrows the abundance and balance of nature:

Where huge ugly office blocks are designed with no spiritual dimension:

Where housing estates are built with no idea of how to create a community, or community spirit:

Where the beauty of nature is neither respected nor appreciated above personal need and greed:

Where there is no understanding of the collective spirit of our land and how we interact with it:

Where the spirits of place no longer have a place.

The key to healing the wasteland is not a mysterious object of spiritual power, a chalice or a stone. It is us.

The human race created the wasteland. Now we must work in harmony with nature to heal it.

We don't need a magic cup, we need a return to an understanding, love and reverence of the natural world around us:

To a recognition and employment of the sacred geometry which underpins the natural harmony and beauty within all of creation:

To an appreciation of spirit of the land, our Mother Earth, and our relationship to her.

The healing of the wasteland and restoration of Albion (the sacred Land of Britain) is therefore dependant on our interaction with the Earth's spiritual dimensions and our re-building and re-connection to their hidden unity; a return to the natural science and understanding employed by the megalithic people and the temple-builders of all ages.

I believe that the Grail Maidens of The Elucidation relate to a time in our distant past when humanity lived closer to nature and we were actually able to see these manifestations of our mythic landscape which are part of the planetary collective consciousness and spirit of the land.

Over time, individual consciousness and the warrior mentality evolved and separated humanity, from nature and from our own nature as connected parts of the collective spirit of the Earth.

So the Grail Maidens could no longer be seen. They became wispy ghost-like apparitions only witnessed by a few.

Since the sixties, the feminine principle has been making its presence felt again.

I believe the Grail Maidens are returning and will be visible again - at our ancient sacred sites, springs, holy wells, streams, rivers and lakes - to those who have the vision and the ability to interact with them.

The mysteries of the Arthurian mythos are a living tradition encoded into our sacred sites and our Visionary Landscape.

The Grail is all around us, invisibly, as the all-pervading planetary life force. Its mysteries are an open secret, permanently on public display in the wonders of nature which surround us.

Even somewhere as down-to-earth as London is full of places where we can sense the air of enchantment and intuitively access the inspiration and wisdom of the Earth.

Camelot Moat is one of them. It is a place of power, a place of visions, a place of healing, a place of other-wordly experiences. Literally.

My personal belief is that is was originally a very ancient sacred enclosure built upon an oracular shrine and holy well.

When you cross the moat onto the island, you symbolically step from the everyday world into the Celtic 'other-world'.

The spiritual realms of the collective subconscious.

Into what I call the Visionary Landscape. Into the mythic landscape. That is where the Grail Castle of Camelot lies, not in the material world.

It is an other-wordly vision. As the Grail always is.

Camelot Moat may not have been the fairy-tale Camelot of myth and legend, created by the imagination of mediaeval Dan Browns, like Chretien de Troyes.

But it could very well have been the real, less glamourous Camelot of an early British Warrior King.

Whether it could ever have been used by King Arthur is open to debate....but it is possible.

The mystics and psychics amongst you may even find it is the location of yet another kind of Camelot, an inner-world Grail Castle.

For the past twenty years, it has been a real and very magical Camelot to myself and to many of my friends.

With this book, I open its enchantment and mysteries to wider public appreciation and enjoyment.

You'll find it is a lot easier to visit than the Camelot of legend.

This one is just at the far end of The Piccadilly Line.

CAMELOT MOAT TIME LINE

Celtic era: Origins unknown, but here is a possibility that this site may date back to the celtic period. The author personally believes it originated as a sacred enclosure, based around a holy well and oracular shrine.

Roman period: Archaeological finds from the Roman period suggest it has been occupied in some form as far back as those times.

Prior to 1066: In the period immediately preceding the Norman Conquest, this site was in the hands of Ansgar, Stalker to the King and in charge of London's defenses. It may have occupied a strategic position in the outer defenses of London.

Post 1066: After the Norman Conquest, William gave Ansgar's lands in Edmonton and Enfield to Sir Geoffrey de Mandeville (the elder). Various references tell us that it was the site of his manor house and folklore records that it was known as Camelot at this time.

11/12th Century: On the death of Sir Geoffrey, the manor and his estates passed to his son, William, then to William's son, another Sir Geoffrey.

1141: Sir Geoffrey de Mandeville the younger is made Earl of Essex by Stephen, during the civil war between Matilda and Stephen. He dies following the siege of Burwell castle in 1144.

The manor and estate passes to the De Mandeville's descendants, the De Bohuns.

1347: Humphrey de Bohun applies to fortify his Manor House at Enfield. I assume it was on the site of the De Mandeville Manor House, some local historians disagree.

1357: Estimated dating for the oak timbers of Camelot Moat's drawbridge. This may have been part of Sir Humphrey's fortification of Camelot Manor.

1380: Humphrey de Bohun's daughter, Mary, marries Henry Bollingbrook, later to become Henry IV. Presumably he knew the de Bohun's manor and estates well. After Camelot Manor's demolition, he made Enfield Chase his favourite hunting ground.

1439: Earliest written record of the name Camelot at this site, sadly, relating to the demolition of "Camelot Manor."

1399: Henry Bollingbroook, then the Duke of Lancaster, creates Enfield Chase, the Royal hunting grounds. Camelot Moat is at its very centre, with four lodges in the North, South, East and West.

1441: There is a written reference to "Camelot Lodge" presumably replacing the manor house. I believe the red tiles still to be seen scattered about the moat date from this building. Bear in mind that the Celtic God Nodens was the linked to the "god of the wild hunt" and is associated with another ancient well once located within the hunting ground of The Chase, within walking distance of Camelot Moat.

1658: A survey tells us the lodge is in ruins, but still shows the name Camelot, both at the moat and in the surrounding area.

1777: King George III leases the park to his physician Richard Jebb who creates the name Trento which became today's Trent Park.

1778: Sir Richard Jebb builds his "villa" on Noddingswell Hill (the sacred well of the celtic deity Nodens ?). Jebb's villa forms the basis of the mansion in Trent Park today. Jebb also landscaped the grounds, creating the lakes.

1822: Camelot Moat features as a location in one of Sir Walter Scott's Waverley Novels, The Fortunes of Nigel. How did Scott know about it ?

1836: The Estate's lease is bought by David Bevan for his son Robert Cooper Lee Bevan, one of the founders of Barclay's Bank. In those days it was the Barclay, Bevan, Barclay and Tritton Bank.

1880s: First excavation of Camlet Moat, by Mrs Bevan, her daughters and their gardeners.

1908: The lease is acquired by Edward Sassoon, whose wife is a member of the wealthy Rothschild family.

1912: Sir Phillip Sassoon inherits Trent Park, along with various other properties, and begins re-designing the house and estate.

1923: Sassoon begins an archaeological dig at Camelot Moat.

1939: Sir Phillip Sassoon dies and has his ashes scattered over the estate from a plane. Trent Park becomes an interrogation centre for high ranking German prisoners of war.

1947: Trent Park becomes a college of Music, Drama and Arts.

1951: The estate and park is compulsorily purchased.

1974: Trent Park college becomes Middlesex Polytechnic, then in 1992, Middlesex Univeristy.

1990: Camelot Moat features in my **Earthstars** book as one of the sites which initiated the discovery - a vast geometric design linking mny of London's ancient sites.

1997: Camelot Moat features prominently in Jenny Lee Cobham's book, **Sir Geoffrey de Mandeville and London's Camelot: Ghosts, mysteries and the occult in Barnet.**

2000: Earthstars The Visionary Landscape updates the Earthstars discovery, expanding the sections on Camelot Moat and the Arthurian mysteries to three chapters.

2009: You are reading it.

Additional photographs

Illustration 39: The Holy Man, Atmachaitanya, leading a Hindu ceremony beside the well at Camlet Moat in the early 90s.

Illustrations 40 and 41: Two examples of sacred landscape art which were created near Camelot Moat's well in the early 90s.

Illustration 42: On his arrival at the moat, The Holy Man began looking for a tree with a Sanskrit Om symbol on it. He had seen this in his vision whilst still in India. He found this OM symbol on a tree near the well. It has now grown out and is unrecognisable.

Illustration 43: Our Lady of Camelot Moat. A statue of the Virgin Mary which was placed at the base of the rag tree beside the well and left there for several weeks until it disappeared.

Illustrations 44: This is the buried remains of some brick or stone structure found in the woods at the corner of Sir Phillip Sassoon's mysterious "Great Pyramid."

Illustration 45: A circle of logs beside Camelot Moat in the 90s, probably used for ceremonies and group meetings. It no longer exists.

CAMLET MOAT.
HOW TO GET THERE.

By Car.

From M25. Take the Potters bar turn off (junction 24) and head down the A111 towards Cockfosters. Take the first turning on the left, up Ferny Hill. As you approach the brow of the hill, you'll see an Egyptian obelisk in a field on your right. About 100 yards further on there is a right turn into the Hadley Road gate of Trent Park. Park anywhere and then find the path which takes you back towards the obelisk (you'll drive across it going into the car park). Fifty yards or so down the path. on the right, you will see the fence around Camlet Moat and should be able to locate the gate to get in.

By Tube;

(This involves a good twenty/thirty minute walk from the tube station, though there is a cafe for refreshments on the way).

Take the Piccadilly line to Cockfosters. Turn right outside the station and walk past the garage, then the cemetery until you come to the main entrance to Trent Park. Follow the drive to the car park and café. On the right of the park café is a path into the woods (you'll be walking up the side of the Great Pyramid here). Follow it through the woods and where it emerges, continue until you can turn left and walk downhill towards a huge oak tree. Follow the path past the oak, then around to the right, past the lakes and up the hill on the other side. At the top of the hill you'll enter more woods and soon there will be a left fork in the path. Take it and walk to the next junction where another path joins from the right. Straight ahead of you, you should see the fence and gate leading into Camelot Moat. Please ignore the information boards. They are not entirely accurate.

Visitors' etiquette:

Like many of the sacred paces in the Earthstars network, there is a special energy at work here which can be a powerful source of healing, inspiration or guidance.

There are no secrets to accessing it.

Just take yourself along to the place, find an accomodating tree to lean against, or a log to site on, then relax

Breathe slowly and deeply; as slowly and deeply as you can - and let the energy of the place gently seep into you, to energise, heal, transform or inspire you.

Simple as that.

I offer one word of warning; If you go in the summer, take some insect repellant. The midgy gnatty things at the moat are voracious, like tiny airborne pirhanas. They're also sneaky so you won't notice the bites till it's too late. Cover up, spray on the citronella or whatever and try not to get chomped.

Light no fires or barbies. Camelot moat is a protected ancient site. You can be prosecuted for causing any kind of damage.

Please don't take anything to leave there. No crystals or candles. Please don't build any more bender shelters or shrines. Let the place remain as natural as possible.

Equally, don't take anything away, unless it is litter or rubbish left by the thoughtless. (Take a carrier bag for that and another to sit on so your clothes don't get dirty from the old logs which pass for seats).

Above all, give thanks and blessing to the spirit of the place for anything you receive here.

Further copies of this book are available to buy on line as a paperback or downloadable e-book from:

http://stores.lulu.com/store.php?fAcctID=4029545

(Just search the title on **www.lulu.com** or Google it. It's easier)

Or see the **London's Camelot** page on **www.earthstars.co.uk** where there is a click-through link.

www.earthstars.co.uk also has details of the Earthstars and Visionary Landscape books by the same author.

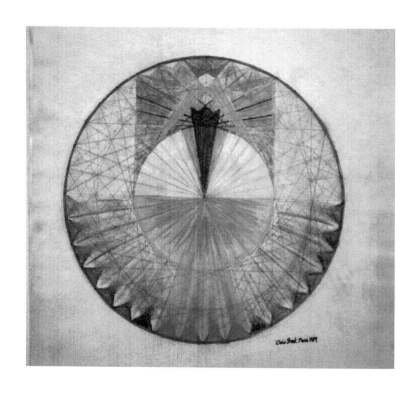

Seek the grail at Camelot.

Give thanks to the grail Maidens

of all wells and springs

and bid them return.

EARTHSTARS PUBLISHING
www.earthstars.co.uk